D1058103

PRAISE FOR *RESURRECTION OF THE WILD*

"Fleming reenvisions how natural history is to be practiced in a rural Ohio landscape that is both wild and settled, both green fields and brown, both indigenous and colonized, both diminished and resilient. Rather than pining for wilderness that has been long lost, the author attends to the regenerative capacities of the land here and now. This book's chief virtue is its detailed fluency in the local coupled with a personal feel for the topics raised. The cyclical time of the landscape—expressed in its seasons and ecological processes—is brought into conjunction with the flow of the historical as framed by the author's personal interactions with the land."

> —**James Hatley**, coeditor of *Facing Nature: Levinas and Environmental Thought*

"Deborah Fleming's warm and wryly humorous persona pervades 'Waiting for the Foal' and other marvelous personal essays about her life in rural southeastern Ohio. Further, broader pieces address the area's history, the Amish community and other unusual people, as well as material threats to the hill country's ecology. *Resurrection of the Wild* will sit on my bookshelf right next to David Kline's classic *Great Possessions: An Amish Farmer's Journal*, for repeated reading."

> —**Carolyn V. Platt**, author of *Ohio Hill Country: A Rewoven Landscape* and *Cuyahoga Valley National Park Handbook*

"Whether writing about her garden, or raising horses, or the impact of coal mining, Deborah Fleming offers an intimate natural history of her farm and her state. By book's end, Ohio is no longer dull, barren flyover land, but one beautiful, fragile web of ecological relationships to which Fleming belongs and is committed."

> —**Tom Montgomery Fate**, author of *Cabin Fever: A Suburban Father's Search for the Wild*

"Every place on Earth needs a writer as attentive as Deborah Fleming, to study it with a loving and clear-eyed gaze. In these essays, she explores the natural and human history of her home ground, the hill country of eastern Ohio, a landscape battered by strip mining, careless farming, and deforestation. Yet wildness persists, there as everywhere, an irrepressible creative force. With a wealth of examples, Fleming demonstrates how nature's resilience, aided by human care, can restore the land to health. May her book inspire readers to join such healing efforts in their own home places."

—**Scott Russell Sanders**, author of *Earth Works: Selected Essays*

"Just as Aldo Leopold chronicles and celebrates the landscape around his 'shack' in Sauk County, Wisconsin, in *Resurrection of the Wild* Deborah Fleming conveys the history and character of her home on eastern Ohio's Allegheny Plateau. This region, like the cutover terrain Leopold calls 'Sand County,' is one in which a broad collapse of agriculture and depopulation of settlements have ushered in a resurgence of forests and wildlife. An elegiac story from one perspective thus becomes a tale of rewilding from another, as well as a field of new opportunities for independent-minded and scientifically oriented settlers. I loved the precise and energetic way Fleming interweaves descriptions of her home landscape's geology, such notable figures from its past as Johnny Appleseed and Louis Bromfield of Malabar Farm, and her own special fascination with horses."

—**John Elder**, author of *Reading the Mountains of Home*

Resurrection of the Wild

Resurrection of the Wild

Meditations on Ohio's Natural Landscape

Deborah Fleming

The Kent State University Press

Kent, Ohio

Library of Congress Catalog Number 2018052635
ISBN 978-1-60635-375-2
Manufactured in the United States of America

Library of Congress Cataloging-in-Publication Data
Names: Fleming, Deborah, author.
Title: Resurrection of the wild : meditations on Ohio's natural
    landscape / Deborah Fleming.
Description: Kent, Ohio : The Kent State University Press, [2019] |
    Includes bibliographical references and index.
Identifiers: LCCN 2018052635 | ISBN 9781606353752 (cloth)
Subjects: LCSH: Natural areas--Ohio. | Agriculturists--Ohio--History.
Classification: LCC QH76.5.O3 F54 2019 | DDC 508.771--dc23
LC record available at https://lccn.loc.gov/2018052635

23 22 21 20 19   5 4 3 2

For my father, Lawrence A. Fleming

Contents

Acknowledgments

Thanks to Dr. Denise Ellsworth, entomologist at Ohio Agricultural Research and Development Center; to Dr. Steven H. Emmerman of Utah Valley University who helped me get my geology right; to David Fitzsimmons, nature photographer, for evenings spent watching the dancing salamanders; and to Irv Oslin, naturalist and reporter for the *Ashland Times Gazette*.

"Falling Rock Area" was published in *Between Coasts*, January 2018.

"John Chapman" was published in *Organization and Environment* 15, no. 4 (December 2002): 475–81.

"Louis Bromfield, Malabar Farm, and Faith in the Earth" was published in *Organization and Environment* 19, no. 3 (September 2006): 309–20.

"Preservation and Freedom" was published in *Organization and Environment* 20, no. 1 (March 2007): 106–9.

"Resurrection of the Wild" was published in *Organization and Environment* 13, no. 4 (December 2000): 486–92.

There will be
a resurrection of the wild.
Already it stands in wait
at the pasture fences.
—Wendell Berry, *excerpt from "Window Poems"*

❧

Wine-hearted solitude, our mother the wilderness,
Men's failures are often as beautiful as men's triumphs,
but your returnings
Are even more precious than your first presence.
—Robinson Jeffers, *"Bixby's Landing"*

Chapter One

Resurrection of the Wild

Ohio Ecology as Regeneration

IN EASTERN OHIO, the northern reaches of the Allegheny foothills rise in a rumpled panorama, tree-covered, with deep watersheds, cliffs, gorges, and narrow valleys. Upper Paleozoic rock layers characterize the landscape: erosion-resistant sandstone forms the tops of higher and steeper hills; lower, more rounded formations indicate softer shales lying near the surface. Seventy percent of the state's woodlands lie in about 30 percent of its area, the unglaciated south and east where the river—called "Oyo" or "Ohi yo" by some indigenous people—bends westward. Growing up in Jefferson County, I believed the state to be a succession of forested hills; in later years, hiking the steep trails of the southeastern state forests prepared me to climb Mounts Katahdin and Rainier.

Still, the state's geological formations are too subtle to be appreciated by those who think only mountains, deserts, and ocean shorelines worth preserving, who denigrate the middle of the country with epithets like "corn belt, "rust belt," "Bible belt," or "flyover land." Years ago a young woman from New York asked me where I was from; my answer, "Ohio," prompted an undisguised sneer. The state contains only one national forest, one national park, no "wilderness." Scott Russell Sanders points out in his essay "Buckeye" that the Ohio landscape does not show up often on postcards or in films (notable exceptions are *Brubaker* and *The Shawshank Redemption*, both filmed partly in historic prisons), seldom even figures in books. The state's location east of the Mississippi and its richness of soil, water, and mineral wealth ensured its early settlement and exploitation, prompting many to dismiss environmental efforts as doomed from the start. Ohio's natural history, however, holds the key to its rejuvenation. As William Cronon argues in "The Trouble with Wilderness," the problem of deleting long-abused land from an environmental ethic means that we idealize a distant landscape at the expense of neglecting the one in which we live, the one we call home.

Ohio contains five physiographic sections. Just under a third of the total area, the unglaciated hill country of the eastern and southeastern counties—called the Allegheny-Kanawha Plateau—is part of a larger division, the Appalachian Highlands, one of the most biologically diverse regions in the world's temperate forests and the most diverse in North America, a fact overlooked by those who dismiss the area as not worth caring about. The Till Plains cover the north, central, and southern reaches of the western half of the state where the soil was formed from glacial deposits over limestone sedimentary rock. Slightly smaller in area than the hill country, the Glaciated Allegheny Plateau angles nearly three hundred miles from Lake Erie's northeast shore to south-central Ohio. Prior to the ice ages, the plateau was hilly and steep; when the glaciers moved southward, they eroded the soft shale in the north, scouring the eastern basin of the lake and Grand River Valley north of what is now Warren. The plateau, while not as dramatic as the hill country, contains some spectacular woodlands such as the Cuyahoga Valley National Park and attractive farmlands in the Amish country of Holmes, Knox, Wayne, Tuscarawas, and Ashland Counties. Still smaller physiographic sections are the Bluegrass and Huron-Erie Lake Plains. Smallest of Ohio's five sections, the Bluegrass extends northward in a crescent-shaped wedge from the Ohio River and includes the Brush Creek drainage area, charac-

Physiographic Regions of Ohio (Ohio Department of Natural Resources, Division of Geological Survey)

terized by hilly terrain and steep watersheds. The section called the Huron-Erie Lake Plains skirts the northern coast from east to west, where it fans out over several counties. Once the site of the Great Black Swamp, a wetland drained by settlers, the western Huron-Erie Lake Plains now include some of the richest agricultural land in the world.

Ample rainfall and geologic history provided the area with a wealth of water—3,300 named streams as well as unnamed tributaries with a combined length of 44,000 miles as well as 50,000 lakes and ponds, abundant ground water, and billions of gallons of water in the wide river and lake that form the southern and northern boundaries. Like most freshwater lakes, Erie is, geologically, a river, which connects Lakes Ontario and Huron. Last of the lakes to be scoured out by the advance and retreat of the Wisconsinian Ice from 100,000 to 10,000 BC, Erie's westerly current runs downhill from Huron to the Saint Lawrence River; long but narrow, its axis parallels strong south-westerly winds, causing the lake to generate violent storms but also to provide summer weather low in humidity. When the Niagara Falls, which are migrating upriver at about one foot per year (they would migrate at five feet per year if nearly half the available water were not diverted to operate power plants), reach Erie about ten thousand years from now, the lake will become a meandering, narrow river.

Prior to European settlement, the state was part of a vast wilderness stretching from the Appalachian Mountains to the Great Plains, an immense and varied temperate hardwood forest containing oak, hickory, beech, maple, tulip tree, walnut, elm, sweet gum, chestnut, ash, and many kinds of conifer. Beech and sugar maple predominated in northern Ohio, while oak forests occupied the south and east, some trees 150 feet tall and six feet in diameter and with lowest boughs fifty feet above the forest floor. The native people fished and hunted deer, groundhog, squirrel, wild turkey, and passenger pigeon. The Mound Builders came in about 9900 BC—about ten thousand years after the first human migrants. At the advent of the European migrations, the Iroquois Confederation controlled the upper Ohio Valley. Drawings at Brown's Island by indigenous people before the seventeenth century show a wild turkey and a goose in flight. Pioneers reported walking for days without seeing the sky and sheltering in hollowed sycamores that grew along stream banks. Daniel Boone is said to have carved a sixty-foot dugout canoe from the trunk of a single tulip tree. The thick canopy allowed only shade-loving mosses to survive on the ground, not the brushy thicket that contemporary hikers know. Indigenous people as well as pioneers hunted the bear, gray wolf, bison, elk, deer, mountain lion, bobcat, lynx, river otter, wolverine, porcupine, beaver, ruffed grouse, passenger pigeon, and turkey. Today, of these species, only deer, bobcat, porcupine, beaver, ruffed grouse, and turkeys remain.

The area once belonged to the Old Northwest Territories claimed by Virginia, Massachusetts, and Connecticut, which deeded parcels of land to veterans of the Revolutionary War. Europeans found their way to it rather late, the first white settlers in Jefferson County disembarking from a canoe as late as 1765. René-Robert Cavelier, Sieur de la Salle reached the Ohio River in 1669, after he had explored some of the Illinois territory where he found large Native American settlements—about forty thousand people. Ohio may have had similar numbers around 1500 BC, but by the time the French arrived, the region—ravaged by war and disease during the previous century—was both heavily forested and sparsely populated.

The very richness of Ohio's resources precipitated its unparalleled exploitation. Ninety-five percent forested at the time of the first settlers' arrival, Ohio was soon denuded of trees. In 1820, 24 million of the state's 26 million acres were forested; by 1883, this figure was 4 million, and by 1940, only 3.7 million acres were forested. The primary reason for deforestation was creation of farms, but arable land too has been lost because of overcultivation, soil erosion, and construction. Twenty-four million acres were in agricultural production in 1900 with rich glaciated soil ranking among the best in the world; today that figure is fewer than seventeen million. Between 1954 and 1992, 28.7 percent of farmland was converted to nonagricultural use. In 1900 urban areas occupied 13 percent of the land they now include. Today farmland is lost primarily to suburbanization due to the aging of farmers and abundant ground water that allows nearly universal habitation.

Still, the state's most profitable resource is neither timber nor soil but fuel minerals, and the primary devastation of the land results from their extraction. Although Ohio's mineral wealth is varied, with deposits of iron ore, dolomite, salt, and limestone, the most sought-after resource until 2011 was coal, lying in rich layers near the surface, where it could be strip mined, a process that is safer for workers than shaft mining but also proves disastrous for ecosystems. After a coal seam is mined, acid mine drainage, typically ferric hydroxide and sulfurous compounds, including pyrite, erode into adjacent land and streams. In the 1970s, acid runoff from mines killed fish populations in Lake Hope in Vinton County and turned Raccoon Creek in Gallia, Jackson, and Vinton Counties orange-red. As a child, I watched hill after hill denuded of trees, terraced by machines large as houses, and leveled like moonscapes. All twenty-five of the most important coal-producing counties lie in the hill country.

The state, with its coal and iron resources, together with its namesake river and lake deep enough for transport, had become a major steel producer by 1890, and along with the devastation of forests and soil came the pollution of air and water, most egregious along major waterways and near cities. Pollution has caused thirteen fires to burn on the Cuyahoga River, the first as early as 1868; one in November 1952 caused the most damage (over one million dollars), but a smaller one in June 1969 was the first to receive national attention. In the early 1960s, biologists discovered that, during parts of the year, fourteen hundred square miles of bottom waters in Lake Erie's central basin were devoid of the dissolved oxygen necessary to support fish populations and that other areas of the lake contained abnormally low levels. Many environmentalists declared that Lake Erie was "dead" and would never again be a viable ecosystem.

Gradually, however, the lake regained some of what was lost. Along with ecologists, fishermen spearheaded efforts to clean up the lake; hunters and trappers—sometimes the bane of environmentalists—helped to protect marshes; hikers lobbied to end clear-cutting in state forests. Pictures of the burning Cuyahoga River published in *Time* magazine in 1969 actually had been taken of the 1952 fire, but the anachronism helped to inspire passage of the Clean Water Act and the Great Lakes Water Quality Agreement. State and national Environmental Protection Agency regulations led to further cleanup of the lake and river, which now support more sizable fish populations. The federal Surface Mining Control and Reclamation Act of 1977 closely followed Ohio rules passed in 1972 requiring planning, environmental impact assessment, and reclamation. In the climate of Ohio, even worn-out, abandoned soil quickly grows up in thickets and woods. Today 6.4 million acres of the state are wooded or forested, nearly 25 percent of the total area. Much strip-mined land has also recovered, due to abundant rainfall, especially in the limestone-rich area near the glacial till. As a teenager, I rode horses and hiked in areas of scrub grasses we called "the strips"; unreclaimed by human beings, the land partially restored itself, first with broom sedge and poverty grasses, then hawthorn, and finally seedling trees. Wild cherry and bigtooth aspen are two species that can return to mined soil. Black locust, which survives on many acidic soils, adds nitrogen. Other trees hardy enough to grow on reclaimed areas include black alder, cottonwood, white ash, white pine, tulip tree, red maple, elm, and sweet gum. Crown vetch, a legume developed in England and said to help replace topsoil, was widely sown in Harrison County in the 1950s. Although invasive, it can be controlled more easily than the thorny stems of multiflora rose— another troublesome import—and helps to prevent erosion on steep banks. Forest restoration takes fifty to one hundred years, but some desecrated soils do recover.

Animals requiring a large habitat such as bear, lynx, and timber wolves are gone forever, but a few species once extirpated or endangered have made remarkable comebacks. Once eliminated from the state by pelt hunters, beavers migrated back into Ohio from Pennsylvania in 1936; by 1961 the number had increased sufficiently to allow for a short trapping season. Although prairie chickens never returned after 1900, the ruffed grouse and quail populations grew. Reintroduced by an Ohio

Division of Wildlife project, wild turkeys proliferated. Bobcats, native to Ohio but extirpated by 1850, began to migrate back into the southeastern part of the state in the 1960s; now removed from the endangered list but still a "protected" species, their populations seem to be increasing: in 2013 the Division of Wildlife reported two hundred verified sightings and recently voted against adding bobcats to the list of "trappable" mammals for 2018. Eliminated from the state by 1900, deer have, as a result of predator depletion and the abundance of field/forest edge habitat, recovered their numbers so successfully that they are widely regarded as "overabundant."

Marsh preservation enabled some water bird populations to recover from the effects of wetland drainage and industrial pollution. At Crane Creek Wildlife Research Station in Magee Marsh, counts in the 1980s revealed dramatically increased populations of black ducks, gadwals, wigeons, canvasbacks, whistling swans, coots, and mergansers. Herons, which numbered 2,200 in the state in 1946, increased their population to 30,000 by 1972. Twenty pairs of Canada geese released in Crane Creek in 1967 became 1,082 individuals by 1972; the geese are now omnipresent. Reservoirs originally constructed to provide water for canals in the early 1800s have been turned into state parks, such as Buckeye and Indian Lakes, and provide homes or migratory rest stops for geese, ducks, and herons. Eagles and ospreys have been successfully reintroduced at reservoirs and reclamation areas. When I was young, I seldom saw deer or hummingbirds and never herons or wild geese, even though I lived in wooded country with plenty of creeks and ponds; now I view them daily in their seasons.

In the Zaleski State Forest in Vinton County, surrounded by the Wayne National Forest, a twenty-three-mile hiking trail stands as a symbol of the rejuvenation of the wild. The poorest part of the state in the late twentieth century, Vinton County was a major iron-smelting area in the early 1900s, even including its industry in the names given to some of its towns—Hope Furnace and Union Furnace, for example. About an acre a day of forest was cut and burned for charcoal, which was used to smelt iron. Named for the French nobleman who financed the land company that built several furnaces, the Zaleski trail fittingly begins at an old smelter. A sign warns "Do Not Climb," but the residue of climbers—paper cups and wrappers—litters the yard.

The hiker quickly leaves behind this testament to human habitation past and present and walks through a copse of massive conifers like ships' masts. Planted by the Civilian Conservation Corps in the 1930s, they grow in straight rows; while some observers find these monoculture forests boring, I love the cathedral-like canopy where I hear not plainsong but the music of the white-throated sparrow. The trail proceeds into more diverse hardwood forests and passes an old cemetery dating from the early 1800s, where headstones lean, names erased by rain and frost. No descendant remains to tend them.

About three miles farther, the trail reaches the level of the old railroad bed and passes a wetland where bees pollinate wildflowers like orange forget-me-not and pink lady's thumb. From there the hiker walks along what was the main road of an old mining town, Ingham Station. During the 1870s, the town had a store, railroad depot, and several houses, yet all that remains is a depression in the ground that was once a cellar hole. Miles along, the hiker traverses an old farm, which again has left no evidence other than castaway foundation stones. Ornamental holly, osage orange, and spruce—often planted to mark the birth of children—thrive, and old fence rows provide homes for quail and other ground-nesting birds.

Less than a mile from the site of Ingham Station, a ceremonial earthen mound gives evidence of habitation by prehistoric people, now referred to as the Adena, who occupied central and southern Ohio in the years 800 BC to 700 AD. They lived in circular wooden houses eighteen to forty-five feet in diameter in fairly permanent villages and grew beans, pumpkins, squash, gourds, sunflowers, and corn, which they stored in pottery jars. Apparently, they traveled long distances in order to trade, for they created ornaments of shells from the coast and copper from the Lake Superior area. Their flint tools and stone pipes have been located as far east as the Chesapeake Bay and Vermont. From their carvings, archaeologists surmise that they honored the hawk and shovel duck. Because of their practice of burying the dead in high earthen mounds, later inhabitants called them "Mound Builders."

They were succeeded by the Fort Ancient people (1000–1600 AD) who built settlements on broad river valleys and lived in rectangular houses. Earthworks that once held wooden palisades surrounding their towns give evidence that they experienced frequent warfare, yet the towns were occupied between ten and twenty years at a time. They hunted and gathered but also raised crops. Some archaeologists believe that they were the ancestors of the wandering Shawnee. In the second half of the 1600s, Ohio was nearly depopulated until woodland dwellers—Shawnee, Delaware (Lenni-Lenape), and Huron—migrated into the state. They, too, used this trail, following the deer they hunted.

After a long, steep ascent, the Zaleski trail passes through an area where the ghostly white bark of birch and beech testifies to the climax stage of a mature forest. Here the hiker finds painted trillium growing near rocks and in the spring sees the lacy white of dogwood mixed with the bright green of early-budding trees. Ubiquitous birdsong announces the mating season. The trail follows an old road that connected two frontier towns whose names recall the encounter of Europeans and Native Americans— Marietta in the east, christened for a French queen, and Chillicothe in the west, a Shawnee word for "village." Settlers used the road until the last of the farms in the area was abandoned in the 1920s. Another part of the trail follows the route of an old road where wagons hauled charcoal to the Hope furnace in the mid-nineteenth century. Both roads had been deer trails used by people of the Fort Ancient and later woodland groups. The roads grew up in grass while the once-planted slopes reverted to woods and then forest. Now the roads are trails once again, traversed by hikers as well as deer. No greater emblem manifests the potential resurrection of the wild.

Wildness is the process which restores and rejuvenates the land. In Wendell Berry's poem "The Wild," the abandoned city lot, although not natural, is nevertheless "wild," and the tanagers and warblers in the locust trees enable the land to remember what it is. Wilderness in Ohio was that canopy under which pioneers walked for days without seeing the sky. Wildness, on the other hand, is the big-tooth aspen taking root on a mined slope. Wilderness was the prairie grass reaching to the saddle horn. Wildness is the dew shimmering at sunrise on the orb weaver's polygonal web strung between stems of Queen Anne's lace, the snapping turtle wading in a drainage ditch, the ironwood tree growing from the cellar hole of a house long abandoned.

The lesson of Zaleski Forest—in which we can observe not only the power of the earth to rejuvenate itself but also the evidence of human life one and two centuries and even twelve centuries in the past—is that we cannot be sanguine about the restoration of forest or farmland. Strip mining continues. More topsoil is lost every year due to construction than to bad farming practices. Industry and development have begun to compromise the water quality of even Big Darby Creek in western Ohio, one of the twelve cleanest waterways in the country and a designated national scenic river. The state's largest stand of old growth forest—Dysart Woods in Athens County—is threatened by longwall mining. Meadowlark and bobolink populations are declining due to habitat loss. Manufacturing, timbering, mineral extraction, and construction interests have powerful lobbies, which impede efforts to preserve forests, waterways, and farmland. Toxic algae blooms caused by agricultural runoff and rising temperatures poison the water in western Lake Erie. In its centennial year (2016), the Ohio Department of Forestry increased logging from 40 percent of annual growth to nearly 100 percent in some state forests. This practice threatens species already rare like the cerulean warbler and wood turtle. As oil and natural gas have replaced coal as the state's most valuable fossil fuel, horizontal hydraulic fracturing ("fracking") poses the largest threat to water, air, and soil quality. In this process—exempted by the

High wall strip mining, Belmont County, Ohio (Photo © Cheryl Harner)

Energy Policy Act of 2005 from sections of seven environmental protection laws—millions of gallons of water mixed with hundreds of thousands of gallons of toxic chemicals are pumped into the ground at high pressure in order to break apart shale deposits and release natural gas. Toxic chemicals from fracking can leak into neighboring water wells, and about 20 percent of the contaminated water flows back to the surface along with volatile organic compounds and radioactive drill cuttings, which are stored in waste pits until they can be transported by tanker trucks and injected into old vertical gas wells—mostly in Ohio. Accidents from fracking sites resulting in contaminated water, air, and soil are well documented in Maryland, New York, and Pennsylvania.

The strength of the eastern deciduous hardwood forest is evident, but whether even second-growth woods will become wilderness depends on the conviction of those who have lived on the restored land and who believe in the rejuvenating process of the wild.

Chapter Two

Walking

"IN MY WALKS, I would fain return to my senses," Henry David Thoreau writes in "Walking." He begins the essay by tracing the etymology of the verb *to saunter*, which he says derives from the word *Sainte-Terrer*, a person who walked about the country asking for charity under the pretense of walking to the Holy Land as did Saint Theresa, and he declares that those who do not go to the Holy Land in their walks are vagabonds or idlers, that all true walkers go forth in a spirit of adventure. Others derive the word from *sans terre* (without land) and Thoreau argues that those without one particular home are better able to be at home everywhere. I agree that true walkers enter a holy land, for they come to know the spiritual as well as visible landscape. The *American Heritage Dictionary*, however, provides the Middle English *santren* (to muse) as the verb's ancestor, and surely to saunter is to muse. We return to our senses when we walk because the human body evolved to walk long distances.

I was nine when I took my first long-distance hike. My family was living in Steubenville, but we drove the seven miles to my grandmother's house near Wintersville at least once a week. I watched the landscape pass—first city, then suburb, then country—and memorized not only the route but also the landmarks. Gradually, I formed a plan to walk all the way from home to my grandmother's, and one Saturday in summer I started off. I was not running away: I set out to see how far I could walk. I covered about five miles before my grandparents on their way home from shopping spotted me and picked me up. I relate this incident only to point out that I was always meant to be a hiker. Even today, I do not know a place until I walk there, until I reflect on what I see, hear, and touch.

The following year my family moved to the country where I had woods and fields to explore. I walked every summer morning before breakfast and learned that the great polygonal webs of the orb weaver strung between high stems and dripping jewel-like with dew foretold several days of fair weather. The prospect of walking to school four miles each way appealed to me, but I never did it because the road to my school had no footpath or berm wide enough for walking. Nor were we encouraged to walk or exercise other than in physical education. My school had no girls' sports teams of any kind, and in those days a girl who showed an interest in sports or hiking risked severe ridicule.

Not until my college years did I become a serious hiker. One rainy day in November 1971, I accompanied a group of biology students who were working for Ralph Nader on an expedition to collect pollution samples along the Olentangy River in Columbus. We tramped across muddy fields and down slippery banks, at times clinging to barbed fencing behind factory walls. The rain and mud did not dampen my zeal to be outside, and a long-dormant need to cover long distances on foot awakened.

Hitchhiking in Britain the summer after I graduated, I discovered one of humanity's greatest inventions: the public footpath. Not only could one walk through the countryside freely, but villages and towns also had well-marked rights-of-way that led to interesting sights and rural areas. Even a large industrial city like Birmingham had public footpaths. Although America is vast, it is very closed off because so much private property is forbidden to walkers. Only in national and state parks and reserves and on the great trails such as the Appalachian and Pacific Crest can people really see much of the land away from the roads. We are "free" in many ways, but not free to explore our environment on foot or even in many cases to walk to work. It may be that city dwellers, by using public transportation, do more for the environment than country people who have no choice but to drive cars and trucks, as buses and commuter trains never serve rural areas. The cities, which seem restricting, actually provide more opportunities than the fenced-off countryside for walking and exploring—or they did before so many cities transformed their downtown areas into cloverleaf interchanges. The movement back toward large pedestrian areas in city centers and reclamation of abandoned lots, railway lines, and canals into parks are two of the greatest national innovations in the last few decades.

For years after growing up, I continued my walks in those woods to the east of my parents' house. In winter the trees seemed all upright trunks, and snow turned the bushes to lace; in spring the dogwood flowered white, and birdsong surrounded me; walking was difficult during summer because branches and brambles sought to reclaim all space; in the most beautiful season, autumn, the maples blazed scarlet and the oaks golden in the cool mornings and warm afternoons.

One summer I started over the hillside with no particular destination in mind. The hemlock, hornbeam, spruce, maple, ironwood, and even the giant white oaks branching above the others were second-growth descendants of the old-growth forest, logged by settlers in the eighteenth and nineteenth centuries. Water flowed over a large rimrock jutting out over an east-facing slope and fell to the stream below, gushing down the hillside all the way to the creek. I continued walking and found a clearing edged by tall white pines standing in a row so straight I knew they must have been planted as a windbreak. Just on the other side I discovered their purpose: they sheltered a picnic house, the remains of someone's dream of a private park, built about twenty years earlier. Swallows and bats had colonized decaying rafters, and picnic areas were now home to rabbits and groundhogs. The white pines soared thirty feet, perhaps fulfilling the dream in a different way than the designer had intended.

Farther down the hillside, a pile of boulders—remains of a bank barn that had stood there perhaps as late as the forties or fifties—provided evidence that the place where I walked must have been pasture. A red-winged blackbird perched on a leaning fence post shrilled its call that sounded like ringing glass. At last finding the creek, I located the big square stones that were the only remnants of grain mills operated during the late nineteenth and early twentieth centuries. The wooden millhouses and paddle wheels were gone, yet locals still knew the valley as Reed's Mills and the stream as Reed's Mill Creek; thus, we know a place by naming it. I felt part of all times at once—the present, when this stream valley seemed a sanctuary from the highways and cities; the moment two decades earlier when a dreamer who might still have been alive conceived the idea to build a private park among the trees; the early twentieth century when everyone's attention was on the Great War, but someone who thought about the future constructed a barn; the middle of the nineteenth century when Reed built his mills to serve a rising population of farmers; the mid-eighteenth century when the first European explorers stepped among massive trees; the early eighteenth century when Shawnee and Delaware hunted deer and bear and believed that streams and lakes held human souls, that larks and thrushes were the living spirits of their ancestors, and that elusive gods walked the land in early morning because they could conceal themselves in the fog.

Across the creek the wooded hillside rose sharply. I recalled the local story that the stage coach from Muskingum had crossed the hills here during the early nineteenth century, and that if you looked closely you could find the trail the old stage road had left among the trees. The creek flowed two feet deep with a swift current; in springtime the water could be as high as three or four feet. Could wagon wheels have forded it? I searched the hillside for any break where people may have built a road. Trees and underbrush hid the stagecoach trail, relegating it to the status of legend, just as they were in the process of pulling down the barn and shelter house so carefully constructed. Thus legends grow not only out of inhabitants' dimly remembered pasts but also out of the land itself.

The sun stood on the tops of the highest trees on the western side of the creek. I turned to retrace my own path back up the hillside, leaving the woods to the chipmunks dashing among the leaves on the forest floor. Entering the deeper woods, I heard the plaintive whistle and chirr of the wood thrush and the clear, three-note call of the wood warbler.

Chapter Three

Waiting for the Foal

As soon as I entered the feed room that morning I knew the foal had been born, because I could hear the stall gate being rattled, and the mare never did that. It was May 19, 1997, and although the foal had been due at the end of April, the spring had been cold, and a mare can prevent the birth until her instincts tell her the weather is favorable.

Because new horse mothers are fiercely protective and will not tolerate dogs or other horses—even stable mates—near their young for several weeks after the birth, I left my dog, Colleen, in the feed room and hurried downstairs with the mare's grain. There on the straw lay the foal, kicking the gate. My other mare and pony gelding stood watching at the far end of the barn, separated from the foaling stall by two gates. Even Soxie, the barn cat, kept her distance, perched on a rafter, but curious nevertheless.

The foal was palomino-tan with a white blaze, black mane and forelegs, and white tail and hind legs, an unusual coloring that I knew it would not retain since almost all foals change color during their early months or years.

The mare nickered to me. When I petted and praised her for her accomplishment, she lowered her head to be stroked; in my experience, all new equine mothers do this, perhaps wanting sympathy for what they have gone through to give me this prize. Equine labor is shorter than women's but more violent. In addition, although delivery is usually less complicated than it is for women, mares have more difficulty carrying the infant to maturity.

My mare was a black Thoroughbred, once a race horse, and, judging from her papers, a successful one. She had been a sprinter— one whose races were mostly under a mile—and had won over two hundred fifty thousand dollars during her career—considerable for the late 1980s. Her neck still bore the semicircular scar of an operation to open her windpipe. Her registered name was Wee Salmon, but I called her Xanadu. The foal's sire, a dapple gray Connemara named Prospect's Callahan, lived on a breeding farm about thirty miles south in Knox County.

I knelt to run my hands over the foal's back and neck. Hoping for a filly, I felt beneath the stump of a tail. No vulva. It was a colt.

The surest cure for disappointment, however, is activity. I fed the other horses to keep them busy while I worked with the foal, kneeling over him and running my hands over all parts of his body, keeping my head well away from his since newborn foals throw their heads up involuntarily. I also anointed his umbilical cord and the bottoms of his hooves with iodine to prevent infection.

Imprinting is the process of handling the foal in order to prepare it to accept human beings. I inserted my fingers into the back of his mouth to simulate a bit, held him around his barrel tightly where a girth will go, and clapped my hands against all four of his hooves to acquaint him with the farrier's trimming and pounding. He did not accept all this attention willingly but struggled against each procedure, at one point even throwing me against the wall and overturning the water bucket. By noon my overalls were soaked and covered with dirt. We went through the entire process eight times with me persisting until his expression changed. I also groomed him, fitted the halter on, and taught him to lead, turn, back, and lift one foot at a time. Part of their training involves acquainting foals with noise so that they will not shy at scary but harmless sounds such as those they might encounter at fairs, horse shows, or race tracks, so I clanged the water buckets together and pounded on the aluminum stall gate with a hammer.

A foal's arrival means a busy day. First I found the placenta for the veterinarian to examine for abnormalities and then forked the straw out of the foaling stall. Foals should be born on straw because it is cleaner than sawdust, but after the birth, any bedding can be used. The mare, too, needed to be cleaned. She showed me her affection as she usually does, by putting her head against my chest.

As I spread the straw from the foaling stall onto the strawberry patch I noticed that another mother had triumphed that morning: three killdeer eggs laid in the vegetable garden on May 7 hatched overnight. Earlier, while I plowed, the killdeer mother stood her ground, shrieking at me and pounding her wings whenever I came near. She never abandoned her eggs, however, and I marked the nest with a surveyor's flag.

A killdeer mother—I don't know whether it is the same one—lays eggs every year, in the garden, in the strawberry patch, or on the gravel driveway because the camouflage is so good. Whenever I hear the killdeer's shriek or see the slender, long-legged, energetic brown bird with white breast and black neck rings, I search out the nest and mark the location to avoid stepping on the eggs. Killdeer young fly immediately after hatching. In this they are like foals, who must get up and learn the use of their legs at once in order to survive.

Because the stallion was dapple gray, I guessed that the colt would become gray as he aged, so I decided to name him Callahan's Grayfell for his father and for the horse in Robinson Jeffers's narrative poem At the Birth of an Age. I guessed wrong: Grayfell stayed palomino-tan for two years and then turned dark bay, more like his mother than his father, although he inherited his sire's striking white blaze and distinctive white legs.

After I had imprinted Grayfell several times, I let him return to his mother and opened the gate to allow them both to walk outside into the paddock. Some of the best moments are those when a foal first leaves the barn and sees how large the world is. Just yesterday he existed only as his mother's second heartbeat. Now he was part of the environment we all share—the emerald-green spring grass, the hills, the blue sky.

On the second day of Grayfell's life, I turned him and Xanadu out into the pasture and watched him running for the first time. In the afternoon, when I brought them back in, we walked around some boards nailed to posts near the barn, which I suspect were once part of a cattle chute, loading bank, or corral. Grayfell, not knowing how to go around, and alarmed that his mother was walking away from him, leaped the two-foot obstacle—impressive for a colt only two days old.

I continued the imprinting process multiple times each day for a week and all summer worked with him for about fifteen minutes several times a day. Foals, like children, have short attention spans and easily become bored with any one task. He was a tough one, more stubborn and willful than any other foal I had ever handled. I began to wonder whether I had taken on more than I could deal with and regretted breeding him in the first place. As the days passed, however, he began to establish his place in the barn and became a personality and presence on the farm. He would be a challenge, but I would learn from him.

Sometimes I feel overwhelmed by how much one has to know in order to keep horses. The best material for stall floors is a layer of gravel underneath packed clay which can be covered with straw bedding. Oat straw is sometimes difficult to obtain, since soybeans and corn bring higher profits to farmers. Moldy straw, furthermore, can adversely affect a horse's respiratory tract. Wood shavings are the bedding of choice for those with plenty of money. Sawdust is less expensive and easier to handle, but it's not as clean or safe: sawdust made from walnut or cherry trees can cause horses to founder, so it is necessary for the buyer to know what kinds of trees the lumber mill uses. My barn has a concrete floor because it originally housed cattle, sheep, and hogs, but bare concrete draws moisture from horse hooves, so I placed rubber mats on the floor and covered them with sawdust made from locust trees. Eventually a layer packed down by horse hooves provided a cushion for the dry bedding which I rake on top. This method seems to work as the stalls stay dry and the horses' feet are in good shape. I enjoy raking sawdust, smoothing it out so that the bedding lies evenly. The work provides an opportunity to meditate while I listen to the swallows in spring and summer, sparrows in autumn and winter.

Owners can't just turn horses out into a pasture but need to know what kinds of grass they are eating. Lush early growth will fatten them up but can also cause laminitis, which often leads to the chronic, debilitating hoof condition called founder, so horses usually cannot be turned out all day in the spring. The new grasses of April and May change in their mineral composition, so the horses have to be allowed to readapt after a few weeks. My pasture is not lush but contains a good deal of sedge grass and clover, which horses do not like. I do not reseed or fertilize the acreage because of the danger of laminitis and because, in spite of the lack of choice grasses, my horses stay fatter than I want them to be.

Horses that are ridden or worked and those with bad feet require shoes, and all horses, even if they have good feet, have to be trimmed, so it is necessary to find a good farrier. People have asked me why domesticated horses need shoes when wild horses do not. The answer is that truly wild horses were small, and their hooves, which grow constantly, were trimmed by continued walking or running over stony or hard ground as they foraged; domesticated horses are much larger and kept in pastures where the earth is mostly too soft to wear their hooves down. Wild horses that escaped from domestication, such as the population in the American West, do not live as long as tame horses and often go lame because of hoof problems. Formerly, as they aged they were picked off by mountain lions and timber wolves, but more recently with the extirpation of predators, they die of starvation since they cannot migrate to new pastures. Most importantly, the horse as we know it has been much changed by human breeding to create a large, athletic animal as unlike its Asian predecessor as the house dog is to the wild dogs of the Eurasian steppes. While many domesticated horses retain the hardiness of their ancestors, many do not—particularly the most finely bred of them all, the Thoroughbred. Many people consider the Thoroughbred to be the most beautiful of all horse breeds, and many are highly intelligent—but they are bred for speed and athleticism while all else is ignored, including temperament and good feet. My mare Xanadu had a fine, placid temperament but the worst feet of any horse I have ever owned, and she was constantly throwing shoes and injuring the pads. Because she raced for an unusually long time, she also developed arthritis earlier than most sport horses do and in her later years became less and less willing to jump or work on the flat. Although I loved her, I will never have another horse with bad feet.

The teeth of domesticated horses need to be filed, or "floated," once a year, due to uneven growth of the surfaces after maturity. A gland in the jowls secretes fluid that cleans the teeth, while grinding grass keeps them level. Horses kept continuously in stalls develop uneven teeth because they never chew their natural food—grass—but instead are fed hay and grain, which are somewhat abrasive. My horses spend twelve to twenty-four hours in the pasture during summer and fall, so their teeth are in good shape. The mare Kestrel lived to be thirty-five, and Xanadu lived to be thirty-one. Decades ago, twenty years was considered old age for a horse, but now many can be active far into their twenties due to the senior equine feeds that have been developed. Wild horses would die of starvation before reaching half the age of well-cared-for domesticated equines.

In 1998, at the annual Horse Progress Days event held in Holmes County, I learned that many farmers have returned to plowing with horses for several reasons: the outlay of capital is smaller than the cost of machinery, they can farm smaller and hillier fields with horses, and there is less risk of injury than with tractors. Using horses for timber-cutting damages the forest floor far less than using heavy machinery.

One farmer claimed that his team of Belgian draft horses could plow a field as quickly as it took another farmer to plow with a tractor, that harnessing and caring for horses took no more time than maintaining machinery, and that using horses was more enjoyable: while working, he listened to birdsong and wind, whereas the farmer on the tractor listened all day to the metallic groan of the internal-combustion engine. A young man raised by countercultural parents who later started a tree nursery farmed his own land with horses in the Maryland hills. Returning to horse-drawn equipment for farming and timbering may be part of the solution to carbon emissions.

I first loved horses (not a conscious decision, as most of our likes and dislikes are not) when I watched two large bay farm horses grazing in a pasture near where my cousins lived in Jefferson County. An aunt and uncle rented a rambling old country house, and when visiting them, we went often to the neighbor's farm to watch the animals. I do not know whether it was their intelligent faces, graceful necks, or sheer impressive size, but I spent a long time talking to them and decided, of all farm animals, I liked horses best, although I loved my puppy and my cat. It was the beginning of a lifelong infatuation. I was destined to become a "horse nut." I am not sure why horse people are thought to be so eccentric while those who devote themselves to tennis, golf, skiing, or cycling are not. Perhaps the unusual zeal ascribed to equestrians is that horse sports are some of the few avocations that require a living partner whose needs are more imminent than the care lavished on sports equipment. Of course, there are aficionados of other animals—dogs, cats, cattle, goats, sheep, racing pigeons—but in no other case do person and animal form a working unit. I love the creak of saddle leather, the sway of a horse's back at the walk or canter, and contact with its mouth through the reins; when I ride I feel that I am part of the horse, more closely connected to the natural world than I am even when I walk. I like driving a tractor, but doing so does not give me the same feeling as riding a horse.

The reason so many women participate in horse sports is that a man on a horse has no advantage over a woman on a horse. Riders do not control horses but harness their energy by working in partnership with them, and women have always had to work in partnership. Except for the tradition of ladies' harness classes, there are no separate divisions for women and men in horse shows as there are in almost all other sports. Women have competed equally with men in all types of riding after abandoning the sidesaddle, and since the middle of the twentieth century women have dominated the horse show circuit. While most jockeys are men, most exercise "boys" and many trainers and grooms now are women.

During my first ten years, I devoted much time to acquiring model horses, reading and collecting horse books, and designing and building my own model horse farm from cardboard. I read every book that had a horse, pony, or donkey on the cover, including the Black Stallion series, Brighty of the Grand Canyon, Misty of Chincoteague, the Flicka trilogy, The Horsemasters, Black Beauty, Smoky the Cowhorse, anything illustrated by the famous Paul Brown, and the greatest of them all, National Velvet, written at a higher level than most animal books. I also read dog and cat books, including The Cat Who Went to Heaven, The Call of the Wild, Lassie Come Home, and Navarre of the North while avoiding anything in which there were no animals. To this day I have never read a Hardy Boys or Nancy Drew mystery. English writers were my favorites because the human protagonist was likelier to be a girl. The beauty of *National Velvet* is that the hero is a fourteen-year-old who makes her own dream come true (she acquires a horse) and then goes on to become a champion (winning the world's most grueling horse race, the Grand National). Although the premise is fantasy, the narrative is rich with realistic detail. It is still one of my favorite novels. Like many horse lovers, I wanted to be a veterinarian when I was young, until I found out that veterinarians' schedules allow them little flexibility. I know several who own horses, but none ever has time to ride. Nor do they have time to write.

I was looking out the window at Xanadu and her foal grazing in the pasture and remembered the spring morning during my senior year in high school when I saw from a window a gray pony grazing in the backyard. In those days I thought of nothing but going to college, but years before I ever had my own horse, I imagined that one might appear on our lawn and that I could keep it. I knew who owned that pony; it had probably slipped through a break in a fence line and traveled about a mile during the night, grazing wherever it chose. We returned it to the owner. Now, watching my own horses, I realize that the dream, once so ephemeral, had become reality. My husband commented that the cardboard farm I constructed as a child bears an uncanny similarity to the place we now live.

Early on I chose to ride in the European style called "riding English"—using the saddle with pommel rather than horn—instead of the American style called "riding western," which is somewhat of a misnomer, as the saddle was designed in Spain, taken to the New World by Spanish explorers, and redeveloped in its present form by Mexicans. My riding muscles have been trained by so many years in the English saddle that today I find western saddles difficult to use. I have attended only one rodeo in my life and amused my relatives by cheering for the bucking broncos and steers rather than the cowboys who were trying to ride them. I admire the reining, roping, and cutting that western riders do since these sports carry on the legacy of cattle ranching but am mystified by western-style classes in which people are judged in part on their fancy, silver-studded saddles, since no reasonable person uses these saddles for ordinary riding. I am also at a loss to explain why women western equestrians find it necessary to wear extreme amounts of makeup, since no one who rides ever stays clean.

From the first, I thought English style riding more elegant and enjoyable, with jumping the skill I most desired to learn. I did not like the artificial, excessive high stepping of Tennessee Walking Horses or five-gaited saddle horses created by weighing down their shoes or the necessity of cutting a nerve in the tail to force the hair to flow in waves. The original Tennessee Walkers were trained to do the "running walk," and three- and five-gaited horses were taught the "slow gate," or "single-foot," in order to allow plantation overseers to travel long distances without tiring horse or rider. (The fifth gait, the rack, is the faster, more animated version of the slow gait.) No one would ever use these show horses now for such practical work. Jumping, on the other hand, evolved from cross-country riding, which in Europe necessitated sometimes leaping over fences built during the time of the Enclosure Acts and the transformation of crop land to sheep pasture. Thoroughbreds and warmbloods are born jumpers, and I wanted to learn to ride in a way that matched their natural abilities.

My first horse was a chestnut American Saddlebred which I owned when I was in high school. Originally trained in five gaits, he was a rescue from an owner who had nearly starved him. He recovered and proved to be a good first horse as he was willing and even-tempered. He had been trained in dressage and sometimes broke into a highly collected canter, a dance in which he changed leads with each step. No one could help me with my equitation as there were no trainers or stables in the county, and certainly few riders interested in the English riding style. Everyone else rode western, and the 4-H clubs were exclusively western, so when I went to the fair I was able to show in only one class and required to ride near the rail (opposite the audience) during the parade because my saddle did not match the others. In most of the country, the 4-H helps young people focus on projects, socialize with like-minded people, and develop confidence. Another equine organization for youth, the Pony Club, is more challenging than 4-H, but it is also more expensive to join.

In the absence of any community, I rode alone near the farm where I boarded my horse, exploring the second-growth woods that covered the hillsides eastward to Cross Creek and Reed's Mills. My horse and I followed a seldom-used gravel lane through woods to a creek bottom and up the other side among fields long abandoned and land that was restoring itself after strip mining. We spent hours every day in summer and weekends during other seasons in those woods and fields. That horse was unquestionably the best part of my adolescence, although he could not have known it.

During my college years and afterward, I took riding lessons sporadically. When I was in my midthirties, finishing a PhD program and in need of activity entirely different from scholarly research, I decided to fulfill my long-delayed dream and took lessons at a stable that specialized in dressage and jumping. "Dressage" is a French word that simply means "training," but equine dressage has as its goal perfect communication between rider and horse. Developed from the training of war horses in the Middle Ages, in which a knight needed his horse to respond immediately to commands, dressage evolved to finely choreographed performance. The highest level includes the airs above the ground of the Austrian Lipizzaner and the Spanish Andalusian horses, but there are many levels for riders and horses less accomplished, including novice, intermediate, and advanced training classes. Although dressage may seem artificial, horses are not asked to do anything that they do not execute in the wild state, and riders learn to communicate with the horse through very subtle movements.

Jumping lessons included stadium courses constructed of rails, gates, and other hurdles set in an indoor or outdoor arena and cross-country courses in which more natural-looking obstacles, such as brush piles, coops, logs, and stone fences, are built in fields and woods. At hunter stables the object is not only getting over the jump but achieving regular stride and creating a perfect arc in midair. I appreciate the naturalness of combined training in which a good jump is one in which no rails are displaced and both horse and rider are together on the other side. Riding a horse over a jump inspires feelings of power, flight, and fearlessness. Even several strides away from the obstacle, the accomplished rider knows whether the jump will be successful. Perhaps pole-vaulters know something of the same thrill. Cyclists know the exhilaration of fast motion through space, but they do not know the exultation of galloping a horse over level or rolling terrain or the feeling of partnership and communication without language. I never pursued the more advanced levels of combined training because riding competitively never interested me as much as riding for fun, so I turned to foxhunting and trail riding. Although formal hunting requires specific attire, and there is certainly a good bit of clannishness among members of older, established clubs, fox hunters seem more genuinely interested in riding for the fun of it and are overall less snobbish than many competitive riders. Trail riding provides the opportunity to see different terrains from the back of a horse and to feel connected to the earth. There is no clannishness or snobbishness among trail riders; people help each other with difficult horses, and I can ride alone whenever I choose.

For eighteen years between high school and the end of graduate school I kept no horse until I bought Kestrel, a chestnut Quarter Horse–Thoroughbred mare, in 1987. She stood 15.3 hands (sixty-three inches at the withers) and had the long neck and rounded hind quarters of a good jumper. I changed her show name, Over the Rainbow, to The Windhover for the bird in Gerard Manley Hopkins's poem by the same name. I used to think that having two names for a horse was superfluous but then realized that just as formal names and nicknames serve to identify us to strangers, acquaintances, and friends, so they do with horses to signify public and private identities.

Herd animals must have companions, however, and some horses refuse to eat if they cannot see another horse. In this way they are like people: even introverted and solitary ones usually need some company. Only once have I seen a horse willingly wander so far from the herd that it was unable to see the others: in 2001, climbing in Nepal above seventeen thousand feet, I glimpsed a lone gray horse of the sturdy variety cropping the sparse grass of the slope. Perhaps he was like those rare people who can be happy entirely alone, such as hermits or frontiersmen.

When I brought Kestrel to our place in Ashland County, she was alone. Turned out into the pasture, she ran the length of her eight-acre pasture, whinnying and working up a lathered sweat. She calmed down in time but spent several months visibly depressed. An acquaintance lent me Shio, a dark bay pony about twelve hands high, formerly a children's hunter who had been without a companion for over a year. Shio was a contraction of his show name, Shy Boy. Newly introduced horses engage in a ritual of sniffing each other's nostrils, stomping and squealing, turning their backs on each other, pinning their ears, and sometimes kicking. This behavior often precedes a period of running together in a field. To prevent horses from injuring themselves, people often stable new horses far from others, then gradually move them closer, and at last pasture them together. Since I was putting a mare and gelding together with no other horses, I let them go into the pasture after only one day of acquaintance.

They bonded immediately. Frequently, when I took Colleen for her final walk of the evening, I saw Shio lying proprietarily in the doorway of the barn while Kestrel lay on folded legs inside.

Kestrel holds an important place in my heart because she was a good jumper and my first horse after adolescence. I took lessons, participated in shows, fox hunted, and rode trails with her. In all those years she ran away with me only once, on a cool day in late fall after she had been stabled for weeks due to bad weather. As she aged, I knew I needed to find another riding horse and bought Xanadu who had been trained in jumping and dressage. Xanadu gave me two foals, Grayfell and Lyric, and so at one time I had five horses in the barn. Gradually, however, the population changed. Shio developed Cushing's disease and had to be put down at the age of twenty-eight. I sold both foals I had bred and raised. Grayfell eventually served the role of clinic horse in Maumee, while Lyric won ribbons as a combined training horse in northeastern Ohio. When Xanadu developed arthritis, I bought Montana, a large (16.5 hands, or nearly sixty-five inches at the withers), athletic, red dun Quarter Horse registered as a paint, to be my lesson horse and fox hunter. Bred in Bucyrus for western-style riding, he had the conformation and stride of a jumper and for a time had been shown in combined training. He proved to be the best jumper and lesson horse of my career and the one who enabled me to do what I most wanted to do—jump obstacles over four feet high in the hunt field. Several years later, I bought a small bay Quarter Horse and named him Dakota; he became my dream trail horse, willing to take me anywhere I asked him to, alone or in company. With his placid disposition, he has the best mind of any horse I have ever owned and has never run away with me. Demonstrably affectionate whenever I walk into the barn, he brushes my cheek gently with his soft nose. When his papers arrived, I realized that he had been bred near Bloomingdale in Jefferson County, where I grew up, so my last horse and I share an origin. Dakota and a borrowed companion I call Maverick, a small bay Thoroughbred retired from racing, are the only horses who now graze my pasture.

Horses in herds, like people in groups, form hierarchies. A mare usually leads, and in my barn that mare was Kestrel. In large horse operations, mares are usually separated from geldings, who will spar with each other if mares occupy the same pasture, but in smaller barns another routine is to pasture mares with one gelding. Stallions in the wild have been described as "herding" and "protecting" their mares or "harem," but this is inaccurate, anthropocentric language. The stallion protects his breeding rights, but an alpha mare always leads whether at the front or from the middle of the herd. Montana dominated inside the barn while Kestrel dominated in the pasture, a direct reversal of the human tendency for the female to be more assertive in the house and the male in public. Researchers have identified seventeen different facial movements that horses use in order to communicate with each other—including opening eyes wide to show fear, raising the inner eyebrow to signal surprise, and pulling back the corners of lips to indicate greeting. They push down the corners of their lips and furrow their brows to express irritation and pin their ears to communicate irritation or anger. In an almost comical gesture thought to represent disgust, they raise their heads and point their upper lips. Stomping a hind leg warns others not to get too near; they indicate dissatisfaction with their riders' signals by flagging their tails or shaking their heads. Young horses spar and play with each other in order to establish their own hierarchy within the larger herd, much as some adolescents dominate others through the strength of their personalities, but in the horse world the alpha mare always governs and sometimes settles disputes arising from the exuberance of youth. In human society, likes and dislikes, joy and anger are social constructs, and I suspect that much more of our behavior is socially controlled than we would like to think. While both social and herd animals form hierarchies, however, I see no evidence in equine herds of the kind of ostracism that people engage in nor the narcissism, egomania, and megaloma-

nia one finds in almost all groups of *Homo sapiens*, the supposedly "wise man."

In natural horsemanship, the human being takes the place of
the lead horse of the herd. Trainers stand in the middle of a round
pen, working the animal at the trot or canter while watching for
signs of submission—cocking an ear, chewing, flagging the tail,
lowering the head—whereupon they look down and adopt a less
assertive posture. The horse finally indicates its willingness to
do the trainer's bidding by walking toward the person, a motion
called "join-up." Repeated sessions are necessary, however, and
neither imprinting nor natural horsemanship can substitute for
long years of work. Training of horse and rider never really ends.

By August of his second year, Grayfell was executing a perfect
collected trot on his own, demonstrating his potential as a dressage horse. One day after I worked with him on leading, right
in front of me he performed a *capriole*, in which the horse leaps
into the air and kicks while suspended above the ground. This
movement of the advanced stages of dressage is executed by
highly trained horses on command but is also performed naturally by young, untrained horses. In Grayfell's case, the leap was
intended to indicate his disdain for me. Foals are like children,
and yearlings are like adolescents: they want to see how much
they can get away with, but they still crave love and attention.

I weaned Grayfell in September because Xanadu was in foal
after I bred her again to the same Connemara stallion. She did
not understand that she needed all her strength for her new
baby and wore a path along the fence trying to get to her first-
born. Shio at first served as a companion, but eventually Grayfell transferred his affection to Kestrel.

One day before my forty-eighth birthday at the end of May,
Callahan's Lyric was born in the early morning. He was coal
black, so I knew he would turn dapple gray like his sire. I imprinted him only four times before he relaxed and worked with

me, indicating that he would be more tractable than his brother. I cleaned out the straw and put it on the strawberry garden, all the time listening to the woodpeckers' drumming, the rattle of the chipping sparrow, and the songs of robins and orioles.

As I led his mother out to the paddock, Lyric whinnied in his squeaky, high-pitched voice. When he stopped to look out over the fields, perhaps wondering at the vastness of the world he had just entered, his mother nickered to him to come to her. He bucked and kicked, shook his head, and then for the first time in his little life, he galloped toward her.

Chapter Four

Wedding Pines

WHEN MY HUSBAND, Clarke Owens, and I first moved to Ashland County in 1993 for my job at a local university, we bought a ten-acre spread in order to stable Kestrel, the one horse I owned at the time. Carved from a larger farm of more than three hundred acres, the place lies in the rolling countryside of Green Township in the southern part of the county. Six miles to the south in Mohican State Park and Forest, the earth convolutes itself into hills and steep watersheds. To the north, the glacial till stretches as far as Lake Erie; southeastward, the once-forested hill country reaches to the Ohio River. The area lies south of the Firelands—about five hundred thousand acres now in Erie, Huron, and Ashland Counties—and is contained in the Western Reserve (part of the Northwest Territories), sold by the state of Connecticut to the US government in the Ordinance of 1787.

In a sense I have returned to a place that I once knew fairly well. Although residents call me a newcomer in spite of my having lived here twenty-five years (it is said that you cannot be a "local" unless your family has been here three generations), I had visited this place many times before and knew the area: as a child with my father I visited Amish farms in Holmes, Knox, Richland, and Ashland Counties; in my twenties I hiked and camped at Mohican and Malabar Farm State Parks and went canoeing on the Mohican River.

We live on a county road of working family farms, although only two of them operate with no second income: a wife and husband run a dairy operation with seasonal help about two miles south of our place; a little farther toward Loudonville a man cultivated six hundred acres mostly in grain until he was ninety-one. He died a few years ago at ninety-two. Although he once told me that if he had a second chance at his life he would not choose farming, I cannot believe he was sincere, since even in his late eighties he leaped with the agility of a young man onto his tractor and with one hand threw hay bales weighing forty pounds high into the mow. His animals and fields were immaculately cared for, and the hay I bought from him was always of very good quality.

We cannot call our place a "homestead" because we did not build the house. Even though we do not cultivate the land and produce crops, I refer to it as a "farm" because we own the house, barn, and two outbuildings of the original farmstead; because the place is surrounded by farms in all directions; and because it is recorded as a farm in the state census. Since ten acres is large enough to be classified as a farm if all of it is tillable or in pasture, every year I am required to fill out a twenty-two-page form sent by the Ohio Department of Agriculture detailing how many acres are in tillage, pasture, or conservation reserve; how many animals I keep of each variety (dairy and beef cattle, horses, lamas, sheep, goats, pigs, rabbits, turkeys, chickens, ducks); how much fertilizer, herbicide, and insecticide I apply annually and in what locations; how much water I use for irrigation and whether its source is a spring, lake, or well; how many bushels of fruit (and what kinds), vegetables, corn, oats, wheat, sorghum, lentils, and soybeans I produce and whether I sell them at farm markets or at auction; how much hay I put up annually and how much I buy from other producers; how many people are resident on the farm, how many of those residents are employed in nonfarm labor, and how many

Wedding Pines, house and barn (Author photo)

nonresident people I hire to work here. I must even record the tonnage of my truck and the horsepower of my tractor. In spite of this chore (which I perform with alacrity because doing so makes me feel important), I do not presume to call myself a "farmer," which is defined as someone who produces more than the family consumes (and incidentally works harder than I ever will). Those whose families consume most of what they produce may be called "gardeners," but that word connotes a grower of plants for sale or designer of landscapes. I am not even a hobby farmer, as I no longer raise foals for sale or sell produce in the farm markets, as I did years ago.

The sense of place here is underwritten by history. In 1812 the Shawnee village of Greentown, five miles west of my house and one mile north of present-day Perrysville, was destroyed by settlers in retaliation for the murder of two farmers. The village (and the present-day township) was named for the Tory Thomas Green who migrated west after the Revolutionary War and lived with the Shawnee. The pioneer horticulturalist and Swedenborgian philosopher John Chapman, known as Appleseed John, lived and planted trees near here.

Our little spread is rectangular, with longer road frontage than depth. The house faces west and sits high on a rise with four large trees in front—Norway spruces about eighty feet high, a cedar, and a pin oak. Two old box elders had to be cut down as they were dropping large limbs close to the house. Tradition has it that the husband and wife who built the original cabin planted the spruces to celebrate their marriage; the trees became landmarks, and descendants named the farm (incorrectly) "The Wedding Pines." I wanted to change it to "Windhover Farm" but finally decided that those trees bear witness to a history longer than ours. The county road forms the border on the west side; beyond it lie the neighbor's pasture and woods. Locals call the road "Honey Creek" because it runs parallel to a stream of that name a quarter of a mile to the east. According to the story, a bee's nest fell into the stream, after which the water always tasted sweet.

To the north a hayfield rises to the neighbors' new house about a half mile away. Separated from the lawn by a line of varied pine and spruce, the bright green of my riding area ends at the border of their thirty-acre hayfield where the alfalfa grows dark green and, just before cutting time, bends like waves before the wind. On the south side, our land slopes suddenly downward into the pasture that takes up most of our acreage. The southeast corner was cut out of the property when the original farmer gave an acre to a son to build a house. A row of tall Norway spruce demarcates the boundary. A spring-fed stream crosses my pasture from the west, flows into a drainage ditch on the township road, and ends in Honey Creek. Our watershed comprises no fewer than 250 acres, so we never have water problems except in the hot summer of 2005 when our cistern went dry and we dug a new well that taps into a deep aquifer. Just below the stream, a small farm pond, originally dug when a pipeline was laid under the lower pasture, is gradually filling in—due, I suspect, to the process of eutrophication. Partially surrounded by cattails, it is home to frogs, turtles, red-winged blackbirds, and sometimes Canada geese. I put up a birdhouse there for tree swallows—the only songbirds, I have read, that will build over water.

The best view lies to the east, where the land slopes gradually toward Honey Creek and then rises again. Trees line the deep, swift-flowing stream that is home to snapping turtles, beaver, great blue herons, noisy kingfishers swooping for their catch, and, in the last year, a pair of sandhill cranes. Long, slender branches of ancient willows with silvery leaves reach to the water's surface. There are eastern hornbeam, American beech, white ash, northern red oak, black oak, sumac, and black cherry, with two massive white oaks reaching above the others. On the far side of the creek, bands of contour-plowed fields measure out the hillside to a township road, beyond which three wooded hills rise. As I walk to the barn every morning throughout the year, I watch the changes the seasons bring—the various greens of spring and summer; the red, yellow, and orange of autumn; the blue, gray, brown, and white of winter.

The farmstead that once boasted at least five outbuildings (verified by pictures taken before the 1960s) now includes only the barn, henhouse, and garage (a converted carriage house). The main dwelling sits on the foundation of a Civil War–era log cabin using some of the original beams. County appraisal forms indicate that the monetary value of the place is difficult to ascertain since there is no comparable property in the township. Although no one is really sure when it was built, the house is dated 1901; wooden pins in the rafters of the upper attic give evidence that the structure is over a hundred years old, and the walls in the living room, upper landing way, and three bedrooms still bear the pegs where people hung their clothes, built-in closets being a later invention. The cellar is a dugout and crawl space where we store potatoes in winter. The tiny kitchen opens into a large dining room spanning the length of the house. The farmwife must have done the extensive canning that would have been required in old days either in that dining room or on the wide back porch that has since been enclosed for a sunroom. An antique Hoosier cabinet that used to stand in my grandmother's kitchen lives there now.

Two staircases leading to the second floor give evidence that the house was probably intended to accommodate multiple generations. One of them leads to an L-shaped landing big enough to house four book cases and an antique wardrobe. The previous owner of the house created a large master bedroom by tearing out a wall that separated two smaller rooms, although he left in place two rough support beams, which, along with two newer wardrobes constructed by Amish carpenters and two old bureaus from my grandmother, give the space its character.

The one-room third floor, probably used as a dormitory-style bedroom for children, contains even more of the history of the house than the other rooms. The chimney, built of brown stone, rises like a pillar in the middle of the room and in the attic takes a nearly right-angle bend. Newspapers that I collected from under the eaves date from 1896 to 1940. Yellowed pages of The Loudonville Democrat from February 6, 1896, tell of O. E. Holley, sent to the penitentiary for two years for horse stealing. Another column on page one describes the Tri-County Teachers' Institute held in the Hayesville Opera House (which still stands) and the program that began with entertainment by the Emerson Quartet and an invocation by Rev. T. Struggles. "In point of numbers," the article begins, "interest manifested and attendance, the meeting of the county institute held here last week was considered the most successful ever held, and Superintendent Scott and his faithful assistants are to be congratulated upon the success they made of the affair." Paragraph three related State School Commissioner Corson's admonition to parents "about what they should expect and what not to expect of teachers": "He said that while many parents could not control one child at home, yet parents expect school teachers to control this one and thirty-nine more. . . . It is much of a wonder that they do as well as they do. He also advised the people to obtain the teachers' side of all controversies, reported by scholars, before drawing conclusions." The quartet and invocation would be absent today, but the message retains its contemporary relevance.

Among the papers, I found editions of The Perrysville Enterprise from 1901 and The Ohio Farmer from 1908. The front page of The Cleveland Press from April 4, 1913, had stories about teachers in Lorain who had convinced police to crack down on dealers who sold tobacco to minors; twenty missing girls—immigrants from Poland, Denmark, Norway, and France, none of whom spoke English—thought to have been kidnaped from a Baltimore & Ohio train in New Carlisle, Pennsylvania, and sold into slavery; Edward S. Smith, former Socialist candidate for secretary of state, who was imprisoned for resisting arrest saying that "the small town police courts" had become "weapons of revenge instead of the tools of justice"; the accidental death of a former Clevelander, Charles Pennington—once a gold prospector in the Yukon and contractor in Chicago—who had entered the wrong apartment and been shot as a burglar; British suffragist Emmeline Pankhurst's sentencing to three years of penal servitude for "malicious destruction of property" in connection with what was termed the "Lloyd George explosion" at Walton Heath; German airmen arrested as spies in France; the impending recognition of the Chinese Republic by US Secretary of State William Jennings Bryan. The house, remote even from small towns, had nevertheless been connected to the world.

The original builders were German immigrants named Weirick, and their old steamer trunk still sits on the third floor. Descendants occupied the farm until the 1960s, and, in a century and a half, only four families have actually owned the place, three of those in the last thirty years. Several visitors have claimed to be descendants of the original owners and live now in Mansfield, Baltimore, and London. They talked about their grandparents' orchards and gardens, outbuildings that no longer stand, and games they played in the barn and fields. I do not tell them of things I have found in the house and barn—children's clothes, a milking machine, broken garden rakes, slats, window frames devoid of glass, old curtains, a plastic dish drainer, even a bathroom sink lying on its side in the attic. I do not mention that every spring on the site where a corn crib once stood I find the detritus of earlier times: pieces of glass and metal, cans, nails—evidence that, as the structure crumbled, its owners used it as a dump. The place would have been the kitchen midden that archaeologists come to study, but I have thwarted them and cleaned it all out. What I could not donate or recycle I burned even as I kept shovels, posthole diggers, old ladders, wooden planks, or wire, which have since been put to use. I do not tell all this to my visitors, however, for they do not want to hear about the changes I have made. They want to tell me what it used to look like so that they might fix in their minds their own pasts. I ponder the question of why these descendants, who seem to care so much, allowed the farm to be sold.

One man who now lives in Mansfield told me he spent many days standing on the front hill overlooking the road perfecting his throw by pitching rocks into the ditch on the other side. Another who lives in London wanted to see the granary where he and his siblings wrote their initials on the walls, which still bear penciled calculations about how much hay was put up in certain seasons. One of our first visitors, also a resident of Mansfield, arrived on his motorcycle and was peering into the garage when I went out with Colleen—who had not yet grown used to strangers—barking and straining on her leash. I asked if I could help him.

"My grandparents used to own this place," he answered. "Calm down."

"I'm quite calm," I replied. "It's my dog who wants to tear your leg off."

He proceeded to get even with me, telling me his grandmother had grown roses where I had gravel and his grandfather had an orchard where I had grass. Most of our descendant visitors are kinder, and recently several thanked us for taking good care of their grandparents' place.

The owners before us (who were not Weiricks) lived here only three years and did not remodel so much as redecorate the house, and we spent our first ten years redoing what they had paid incompetent contractors to complete. We replaced the house and barn roofs, both furnaces, and the shower; insulated the attic; and installed new double-pane glass in each of thirty-two windows. I spent many hours stripping purple, iridescent green, and flowered wallpaper from living room, master bedroom, and study walls while Clarke read aloud to me. I had learned the technique of stripping wallpaper from our first house, also a fixer-upper, in Granville, in Licking County, but had not been prepared for six layers that I removed from the back staircase of our present house. It was worth the work, but to this day I cannot look at wallpaper anywhere without wondering what poor person will be stripping it off after twenty years.

Realtors advise buyers of old houses to expect to spend another 40 percent of the purchase price on upkeep, an adage which has proved in our case to be accurate. At the same time, well-maintained older houses tend to hold their value longer than newer ones. I feel that the house talks to me, telling me what it needs to stay sound, but not always in language I can understand. It resembles a living thing for which one change affects all other parts. We discovered, for example, that leakage into the second story had been caused by water vapor condensing not on the roof, as in the old days of coal-burning furnaces, but inside the chimney because newer, more efficient gas furnaces do not lose as much heat as older ones that would have forced humid air outside the chimney. Birds had also built nests inside the chimney, eventually blocking some ventilation. We solved the problem first with chimney liners and later with a high-efficiency furnace vented out the side of the house, but when I tried to discover why the leaking had not happened when the gas furnace was first installed, no technician could answer. A colleague of mine who teaches philosophy and who has worked on his own house asked what else we had done that might have caused the condensation. We solved the mystery:

by replacing the old windows we had eliminated air leakage on the third floor which had previously carried away the water vapor. Technicians provided the solution, but it took a philosophy professor to explain the reason.

The garage has undergone a transformation as well as the house. Its sliding wooden doors refused to budge when the foundation settled. I hired a carpenter to build new doors, but when a storm in 2009 blew the entire structure off its foundation, we knew we were in for some major renovation. The structure, it seems, had not been grounded or cabled properly. When the contractor dug out the foundation, the concrete floor buckled, and we were in for even more repair. The finished garage, grounded and cabled, sports two state-of-the-art spring-loaded doors.

"You've moved up in the world," a visitor remarked.

"My bank account hasn't," I replied.

Most of our furniture is old, much of it inherited from my parents and grandparents, all of whom were antique collectors. The house I grew up in, which my parents occupied for forty years, was also an original farmhouse, although it was not as old as the one I live in now. The wardrobe, according to the story, traveled disassembled in a wagon over the Cumberland Gap, but this could not be true as their ancestors migrated across Pennsylvania. Our dinner table and a china cabinet served my maternal grandmother's family for sixty years. Our bedstead, from my Grandmother Fleming's house, was the guest bed where my sister and I slept when we visited as children.

Both sides of my parents' families, descended from English and Anglo-Irish immigrants in the eighteenth century, seem to have come from Massachusetts, my father's paternal ancestors having originated in East Anglia and Worcestershire and having traveled west after the American Revolution because of their Tory sympathies, his maternal ancestors (named McKirahan) having emigrated from County Wexford, Ireland. The two sides of his family were farmers in Jefferson and Logan Counties. His mother lost her father when she was eighteen to the flu epidemic at the end of the Great War. The only photograph I have seen of her when she was young shows a very beautiful woman with a thoughtful expression. Her widowed mother worked as a janitor to support two daughters, both of whom obtained teaching licenses from Miami University when one year of study was sufficient to teach elementary school. The younger daughter stayed in Logan County and eventually married a farmer; my grandmother taught school near Steubenville while she completed her degree at Kent State during the summers. Her marriage to my grandfather ended her career since the school district in those days did not allow married women to continue teaching. The son of a farmer turned dairyman, my Grandfather Fleming was one of the early flyers of single-engine propeller-driven airplanes and transported mail until he lost his plane in the Depression. I still have the cap, scarf, and gloves he wore when he flew and a picture of him as a young man wearing jodhpurs. On the transept over our kitchen door I keep a quart-sized glass milk bottle with a cardboard cap that reads "J. W. FLEMING AND SON, 3% BUTTER FAT OR MORE, FOR BABIES AND INVALIDS, SEAL KAPS PAT NOV. 2, 1920, OTHER PATENTS PENDING," all that remains of the dairy also lost in the Depression. Nearby sit three other antique glass jars, none so venerated as that one, probably blown in one of the factories along the Ohio River that used to produce the famous Fort Steuben glass.

The family of my mother's paternal grandmother migrated down the Ohio and Mississippi Rivers on a raft and ended up in east Texas. The other branches of my mother's family traveled southwest to Bell County, Texas. Her parents met there and moved in 1920 to Ohio to find work in the factories. Both had grown up in the country, my grandmother on a farm that produced cotton and sugar cane and my grandfather on a goat ranch. The only famous person among all relations I have ever discovered was my maternal grandmother's second cousin, the most decorated soldier of World War II turned actor and songwriter, Audie Murphy.

When my parents retired and moved from their house, I inherited many books and boxes of letters, primarily because I was the one who had space enough to store them. As I delved through the contents, I felt like an anthropologist discovering cultural traditions of bygone times. Among my father's things I found a watch engraved with the name "Oral Windham," my great-grandfather who died in the influenza epidemic of 1918. In the closed library shelves on the landing, I keep antique books that tell a story not only about one family but the times they grew up in. Grandmother Fleming's copy of *David the King*, published in 1946, cost seven cents to mail from the publisher. In another book of hers, the *Jones Third Reader*, she practiced her beautiful penmanship with round flourishes in capital letters as she wrote her name, Eulah Windham. The book's history was inscribed on the inside front cover: "bought Sept 13, 1910" and "bought Jan. 18, 1911, age 8 years." Published in 1903, the year of her birth, the tome had apparently lasted through eight students. Among the other books is *Peck's Bad Boy Abroad*, published in 1905 and given as a Christmas present to my grandfather "James Harlan J. Fleming from his friend Perry B." The pages of a copy of Hawthorne's *Twice Told Tales* are brown with age but bear no date; the book is stamped with the name W. W. McKirahan, my great-great-grandfather.

Other books, of unknown origin, include *Fern Leaves from Fanny's Port-Folio*, a collection of sentimental short stories by an author calling herself Fanny Fern and published in Cleveland by the Burrows Brothers in 1882, and *Pearls of Thought* by Maturin M. Ballou published in 1880. This one turns to be a dictionary of words like "knowledge" and "discernment" and definitions from great writers such as George Eliot and Leo Tolstoy. I wonder whose hands in what year placed the red maple leaf I found tucked away between two pages. There are several old Bibles with tattered black covers. Books inscribed by my father include the illustrated *Treasure Island* published in 1911 (fifteen years before he was born); *John Martin's Big Book*, published in 1931; *Modern Story Book*, also dated 1931; *The Dog Book* by Albert Payson Terhune (author of *Lad: A Dog*), published in 1932; *Children of Other Lands*, sporting a drawing of an Arab boy on a horse,

dated 1933; and *Last of the Mohicans*, published in 1938. He took
good care of his books and toys, as I also inherited one of his
trucks and a model plane. I have my mother's 1949 copy of *War
and Peace*, the edition I first read when I was fifteen.

Besides the books, I found a *Christmas Ideals* magazine from
1959; a coverless book about surveying; *Yankee* magazines from
the 1940s containing a good deal of war propaganda; 1951 Ayr-
shire breeders' manual; a pamphlet dated 1937 on the history
of the Northwest Ordinance; *Holiday* magazine from 1949 fea-
turing articles on horse racing; a commemorative issue of *Time*
magazine with Native Dancer on the cover dated May 1959;
and *The Farm* quarterlies from the 1940s and 1950s, including
one from 1953 with an essay by Louis Bromfield whose Malabar
Farm is six miles to the west.

One gem that gives me a window into the past is *Sheldon's 20th
Century Letter Writer*, "an up-to-date and accurate guide to correct
modern letter writing," dated 1901 and inscribed in beautiful
calligraphy by my great-grandmother Alice Grafton Fleming.
The introduction includes advice on punctuation, grammar,
titles, contractions, capitals, penmanship, postscripts (to be
avoided unless absolutely necessary), style ("Natural language
and originality of sentiment are all that is required in good letter writing"), and even posture: "The POSITION which you as-
sume in writing is very important. To bend or contract the body
is both inelegant and injurious. Sit erect and let your paper be
before you, slightly to the right. . . . Do not touch the pen itself
with the fingers, but allow the ball of the index finger to rest
lightly about half an inch from the point of insertion of the
pen into the holder." The different chapters present examples
of types of letters which the writer should follow: social and
family epistles include "Letter from a Mother to her Daughter
at Boarding School" and "A Brother's Warning to a Sister," alert-
ing her to the ignoble character of a man with whom she had
gone out riding; missives of condolence, congratulation, and
introduction (including "One Lady Friend to Another" and "A
Hero of the Spanish-American War to the Secretary of War");

love letters, such as "A Declaration of Love," "A Second Attempt to Win a Lady's Favor," and "To a Lover Who is Dissipated"; wedding announcements, valentines, invitations (even a special form for an invitation to a German), acceptances, regrets, notes of ceremony and compliment; business letters; miscellaneous (such as asking a friend for a loan and requesting a salary increase of an employer); and letters to publishers from both professional and amateur authors.

The examples are exhilarating. "Introducing a Coachman to a Prospective Employer" contains the information that "The bearer . . . has been in my employ for two years and has always given entire satisfaction. . . . I recommend him heartily as a good driver and one that is kind and faithful to horses." "On the Marriage of a Bachelor" begins "The tidings of your marriage were wafted to my ears an hour ago, and now that the spasm of surprise is over I am beginning to realize the full meaning of what has happened. I congratulate you with all my heart, while I look at you in awe. How in the world did you ever manage it, old fellow? . . . do tell me, 'pon honor, have you been obliged to quit smoking, or does she allow you to still enjoy your weed, and in the glory of her presence?" A letter of condolence on the loss of a fortune conveys the sentiments, "I am deeply grieved to hear of your loss, but bear up, old man; there is a good time coming; you are still but a young man, and pshaw! what is money? . . . surely the care of such a fortune as yours must have been very wearying." If these letters are to be taken as satirical, a love letter from a soldier ordered to service is not; he writes to his beloved that he is to be sent to Cuba, for when the book was published, the last conflict the United States had been involved in was the Spanish-American War. I try to imagine the world my great-grandmother inhabited, and indeed my grandparents for a short time, without the two great conflicts of the twentieth century, the Holocaust, space exploration, and the Civil Rights movement. The great enemy was not Germany, Japan, the Soviet Union, China, al-Qaeda, or the Islamic State, but Spain.

The real epistles tell other stories. My mother saved the correspondence of four generations of her ancestors whose names
I had never heard of and who lived in Oklahoma and Texas. The
letters date back as far as 1887 and often begin in the style of the
time such as "Mother, I take pen in hand to answer your kind
letter of March 11. Please let your heart be eased with the knowledge that I, your fond son, am well." I found envelopes as small as
three by four inches with stamps costing one and two cents and
addresses giving name, town, and state only. One folder nearly
disintegrating with age contained the deed, title, and tax statements of my great-grandfather's ranch, along with accounts—
dated in the 1940s—of several purchases of additional acreage.
(Reading it, I wonder how my great-grandmother felt when her
husband sold the homestead they had built together—whether
she regretted it, as my Weirick visitors seem to do, or whether
she was relieved that they no longer had to work hard to wrest a
living from the land.) My mother's paternal great-grandmother
seems to have been something of a hypochondriac. Letters to
Mrs. S. E. Sparks of Bell County, Texas, on stationery of the
Lloyd Chemical Corporation of Saint Louis diagnose illnesses
she described by letter and prescribe medicines they sold, such
as Alaxo for constipation. None of these people, whose voices
are now silent, could have known that a descendant they never
knew would read their correspondence one hundred years later
in a farmhouse in the Ohio countryside and wonder about the
absence of laws against pharmaceutical misrepresentation.

Voices still speak to me from my mother's diary of the war
years in which she records the progress of the Allied forces
against the Fascists. Another diary, written by my father's aunt
on note paper, includes her descriptions of travels to the Se-
wanee River, Appalachian Mountains, and Virginia. The person
I knew as eccentric, xenophobic, and racist had also been a lover
of nature, an environmentalist before that word existed, who
worried that pesticides might kill the honey bee population and
oysters in the Chesapeake Bay. In spite of her prescient concern

for the earth, she and her husband, a physician, sold the mineral rights of their farm in Jefferson County, which was subsequently strip-mined and then turned into an industrial park.

Family photographs preserve a kind of history with their visual narrative of the transformation of individuals, but also of families. One shows a set of great-grandparents surrounded by six children with spouses, their eleven children and spouses, and thirty great-grandchildren. Studying it, I am aware of a strong sexuality pervading the record of a family reunion. At the same time, I ponder the illusion of unity represented by photographs: in this picture, as in most, almost everyone is smiling, yet I know that conflict, more than harmony, shapes and reshapes families and generations.

Not hoarders of new things, my mother, father, and grandparents were nevertheless compulsive savers of old things besides letters, books, and antiques; their houses were always filled with clutter, including many items they never used. (As a result, I am a compulsive organizer and value space on which I can lay a book, open a newspaper, or set down a burden.) The slogan "Waste not, want not" characterizes the saver's ethos, but the feeling goes deeper than that. I do not remember a single visit to my maternal grandmother that I did not hear about how hard things were in the Depression of the 1930s. She never mentioned the Great War that raged during her adolescence, claiming on the contrary that those were her best years, and seldom talked about the Second World War except to describe the food rationing. Grandma Fleming, on the other hand, never talked about the Depression or either war but often mentioned that when she and her sister were children they received only one new present each (at Christmas) and one new dress per year. Her back staircase was so full of packed boxes that it was nearly impossible to climb the steps. The impulse to save may go further into the psyche than memories of subsistence farming. I suspect that keeping things, with the claim that one day these items will be needed, is a way of hedging against the one inevitability of life, as well as storing against ruin.

Clarke and I do not hoard, but we reuse or recycle all we can. When wheelbarrows rust out, I take them apart and employ the wooden handles as tomato stakes. Old sheets and towels beyond mending become cleaning rags. Torn quilts and blankets cover saddles in the barn. Nevertheless, in emptying out trunks and boxes, donating things we don't use, and organizing file cabinets, I acknowledge my mortality. Sometime I will not need these things, and someone else will have to deal with them. We are known in part by what we leave behind.

Set back from the house about a tenth of a mile from the road, the Dutch-style bank barn, called "fore-bay" by agrarian architectural historians, is literally built into a bank, the upper story reaching out over the lower one. It faces east toward the sheltered side, as the weather always comes from south, southwest, or west, and occasionally from the north, but never from the east. Long metal pipes reach not through the great beams holding it in place, as with the carriage house/garage, but from underneath the barn far into the ground on the upper side to stabilize the structure and keep it from falling forward. The foundation is made of indigenous stone, the upper part local wood. The builder meant for it to last: every carpenter I have hired reports to me that it is well built, having twice as many beams as would have been required. Those beams still wear their outer bark. Inscribed on foundation stones are the year 1878 and the name of the original owner, Weirick. We have replaced aluminum downspouts with steel and the original slate roof with tile; upgraded all electrical wiring and lightning rods, and had the whole barn painted dark red. Otherwise, it remains unchanged.

The hayloft takes up most of the upper story and could hold an estimated three thousand bales. Even when I had five horses, I did not put up more than several hundred, so I use the rest of the space to house equipment. The third level I leave to the bats and owls that occupy the high rafters, although one summer I mustered the courage to climb up there to sweep out old hay and guano. A hay rake still hangs suspended from the highest rafter, left over from the days when this farm was several hundred acres in size and produced enough to feed a herd through the winter. Narrow gaps separate the boards to allow air to circulate around hay, which if wet or even moist can generate heat and cause fires.

The feed room sits underneath the third level at the front of the granary where five stalls indicate that oats, wheat, and corn were probably the main source of livelihood for the farm. I have turned the granary into a tack room and storage area for cat food, bird seed, and anything else that must be locked away from raccoons. There I store an army saddle dating from the Great War and an ice cutter and old weigh scales left over from my Grandfather Fleming's hatchery business, which failed in the 1960s. Hay forks, a potato fork, and several hoes and rakes that I still use came from my great-aunt's basement where she kept them after her father gave up farming. I also have his collection of wooden-handled tools. They remind me of generational continuity and the fact that, while many farming methods have changed, many have not, as I do much of the work on my place by hand.

Wooden stairs lead from the feed room to the lower level where the horses live. A raised concrete dais extends more than halfway down the middle, from which the farmer would have fed cattle or hogs in troughs along the side. Six double doors look out toward the east. Instead of building stalls, I put up gates, which I close only when I need to separate one horse from the others; most of the time the horses walk about freely.

Once, a woman came to ask my husband whether we would allow our barn to be part of a self-guided agricultural tour. People came every year from several states to view the barns of Ashland, Richland, and Wayne Counties. They wanted to feature ours because of the granary. My husband told her, "You will have to talk to my wife. That barn is her baby." She remarked to me that the old-growth forests of Ohio are contained in its antique barns. Although ours did not become part of the tour, I hope I am preserving something of the state's ancient heritage.

When we first moved north from Granville, I paid an acquaintance to trailer my mare from the place where I boarded her to our new farm. Getting out of his truck, he remarked, "Boy, Debbie, when you move to the country, *you move to the country.*" We are six miles from the nearest market, three miles from the nearest encampment where there is a post office, and fourteen miles from the nearest settlement that might be called a town, yet the traveling purveyors of religion find us out regardless of how far out of the way we live.

The first time an evangelist strode across the lawn it was summer, and I had just dragged the rototiller out of the garage. The elderly but spry and determined woman opened her Bible and read a passage about people being punished with war and plague.

"Now doesn't that sound like today?" she asked.

I disapprove of scholars and intellectuals putting these people down with their superior knowledge of Biblical exegesis, and I was flattered that anyone cared about what I thought, but I wasn't going to be preached at.

"It sounds to me like thirteenth-century Europe," I remarked.

"But doesn't it also sound like today?" she persisted.

"I don't know of a time in history when there wasn't war and disease," I answered.

"Don't you think it might be a wake-up call to the people of today?" she countered.

I made excuses about having chores to do, and she left.

The second time, the preacher brought reinforcements. Four women of ages representing adolescence to veneration drove up to the house, parked, and walked to the door. I saved them trouble by suggesting immediately that they work on more promising souls.

The third time, a well-dressed, good-humored woman approximately in her forties came to the door and greeted me exuberantly. She wanted to talk about something, she said, and reached into her voluminous bag.

"Is this about religion?" I asked.

"Yes," she said cheerily. "Does that bother you?"

Her optimism and friendliness were too much for me.

"I'm an unregenerate heathen savage," I replied, smiling. "I'm a hopeless case, and you will never succeed."

As she walked away laughing, I wished she would convey my message to all her confederates who would know that at my house they would not find a soul ready to be saved. I did not want my soul to be saved, and I would not let them save it no matter how hard they tried. I wanted it to stay here with the great blue herons, eastern box turtles, and tiger swallowtails. Nor would they enlist me in their fight to save the human race, as I did not think the human race worth saving.

The fourth time occurred on a late-summer Sunday morning after I had ridden my horse and then picked tomatoes under a slightly overcast sky amid the warm breeze of early autumn. The world could not have seemed more beautiful when an immaculately clean Buick full of people pulled into the driveway, all the way down to the end near the garden. A well-dressed woman got out and stepped toward me with caution as she was wearing high heels, which do not work well on gravel.

"Do you need directions?" I asked naively, ready and wishing to be helpful in those pre-GPS days with all I knew of the scenic township roads roundabout. When she pulled a copy of *Watchtower* out of her bag, I suggested that she go away. I was disappointed that I had not been able to be helpful and mystified that she felt impelled to educate strangers in the religion that already dominates the culture rather than showing by example and sharing her considerable resources with people in need.

One day the disciple was a man who came to the house and was greeted by Clarke who has a quicker wit than I do.

"Jesus is coming," the man began.

My husband countered with, "Tell you what: if you see him, you let me know. Or if I see him first, I'll call you. What's your phone number?"

The disciple turned on his heel and hastened toward his Thunderbird.

My last visitor (and it has been a long time) was a pleasant-looking elderly lady who came not to the side door, as most people do, but to the front. A car waited for her beyond the mailbox on the county road, where cars travel infrequently but swiftly, and a driver heading south cannot see the driveway from beyond the rise.

She wished me a nice day. "We're visiting people who might not know about the love the Lord has for them," she said sweetly.

"I know about it," I answered. "By the way, you might not want to park your car on that road. The pickups fly pretty fast over those hills."

"With all the problems in the world today," she persisted, "we want to show people a way to change it."

"I like the world well enough the way it is," I replied. "I wish people would stop trying to change it." The poor woman looked troubled.

"I'm a pantheist," I explained, trying to save her time. "I honor solstices and equinoxes, sunrises and sunsets, the phases of the moon. Everything is God."

Looking perplexed, she told me her name and headed toward the car where her companion waited. As they drove northward, I felt downcast that I had disappointed yet another would-be missionary. Then I realized why these people inspire in me a feeling verging on resentment: they are not interested in me but in themselves; they do not knock on my door to meet and talk to me but only to convey their version of what other people should think. If some itinerant, leather-clad John the Baptist walked from the coast bringing news of conservation easements or John Chapman emerged from the woods teaching the philosophy of Swedenborg, I think I might listen. My miracles are the constantly changing clouds driven eastward by the wind, fruit ripening in late summer, rain filling streams and ponds, butterflies tugging nectar from blossoms, gray features of the moon looking on the earth as it has done since long before people ever stood upright and dreamed their anthropomorphic gods into existence.

Pictures of the farm taken in the early nineties show small trees and wide expanse of grass behind the house. Now the lawn is mostly shaded with white pine, locust, cottonwood, birch, walnut, maple, blue spruce, and hemlock. The windbreak to the north of the house contains a double stand of blue spruce, red spruce, and white pine, three feet high when we moved here and now thirty feet high and cacophonous in spring with sparrows, wrens, robins, and orioles and in fall with sparrows and woodpeckers. Although twenty years are a long time in the life a person, they are a mere second in the life of the land which owns us more surely than we will ever own it.

Belonging is not a static but an active state achieved through the small tasks of daily life as well as the larger ones—mucking out stalls, raking leaves, cleaning the house, making the place daily more mine than any printed deed in the county courthouse can. The land has also come to know my being and habits; although we have our differences, we communicate in a grammar of intimacy. At the edge of the garden are stones marking the graves of twelve cats. Colleen is buried beneath a rectangular limestone slab shaded by a white pine. Shio, Kestrel, Xanadu, and Montana are buried at the top of the hill in the pasture, their graves unmarked except for the milkweed and thistle that regenerate every summer. Still, the place was also home to pioneers and generations of Weiricks who farmed the land, as the trunk in the attic testifies. The detritus of their habitation still rises to the surface with the spring thaw. I am more caretaker than owner. Whoever occupies this place when I have gone will change things but will also be a traveler as well as inhabitant.

Chapter Five

The Garden

"LANDSCAPE PROVIDES OUR first geography," writes Maxine Kumin, "the turn of the seasons our archetypes for our own mortality." The land bears witness to the history of a place. Human beings change it, but the earth changes them more profoundly by forcing them to adapt to weather, climate, soil, and rainfall. There is nothing subtle about the seasons in Ohio, not only the temperature but the humidity, wind, slant of light, feeling in the air. I am not like a migrating bird; I like to live the entire year in one place, to watch and feel the seasons passing and one year becoming another.

Seasons are much subtler in places like California. A native of upstate New York who spent years in southern California told me he believed that pitting oneself against the weather is necessary in order to stay sane, that in climates where people are not challenged by weather, they turn their struggles inward. While northerners complain of long cold winters and deep snow, dealing with the elements forces them to engage with the world, even though the Industrial Revolution compelled most of the population to leave the farm to find work. It was the first time I ever considered that shoveling snow might be salubrious. It seems to me, however, that every climate engages inhabitants in some way with weather.

Spring in northeast Ohio has at least three subseasons, the first beginning around the third week of March, when daytime temperatures rise but nights can still be cold, sometimes well below freezing. My first task of the year is to prune the old wood from the blueberry bushes and spread mulch at the base. I clear the garden of winter debris, dig out corn stubble grown soft in winter mud, and cut back last year's asparagus stems.

The second phase of spring begins in early or mid-April when temperatures can still fall below freezing, especially at night, but a wet, earthy smell and a feeling in the air alert residents that life is ready to break out of the soil. Then the grass begins to grow, about the third week of April, when there may still be snow on the ground. Early grass is a beautiful lime green, which it will never be again during the year. Crocuses bloom, usually only for a week. As crocus petals turn brown and fall off, the bright red tulips open, followed by sun-yellow daffodils, then deep purple hyacinths, and finally royal purple irises in my rock garden on the south side of the house, which receives the most sunlight.

As soon as the soil is dry enough in April, I plow and cultivate the vegetable garden with a rototiller and transfer the horse manure from a mound I nicknamed the Cascade Range. Having had all winter to decompose, the compost is rich and black. Organic matter is fully composted when its original components are unrecognizable. Using a wide-tined steel fork, I shape and sculpt the mound that is about thirty feet long, four feet wide, and three feet high. Attacking the manure pile always appears to be a bigger job than it finally is; I enjoy turning it several times a year, rotating it so that all parts are oxygenated. I spread the manure with my wheelbarrow along and between the planting rows and immediately begin building a second mound I call the Coast Range which will become next year's compost. We throw food scraps onto the manure, as well as shredded leaves in the fall. The agent at the Agricultural Research and Development Center in Wooster where I had my soil tested reported to me that it was very rich. After twenty years of fertilizing the soil, I can cultivate the humus to nearly a foot of depth. Many organic gardeners will not use rototillers, as turning the soil so deeply brings weed seeds to the surface, yet the tiller also aerates soil and aids in decomposition of compost. I find that raking by hand and rototilling take about the same time and result in similar growth of weeds.

At the north end of the garden, walnut, maple, and spruce seedlings my father gave me years ago grew too big to be transplanted and now form a small copse. Once I had planned an orchard there, but the spring frost killed my cherry trees. I replanted, only to find deer browsing them in the spring. Tree bonnets protected the leaves, but in the fall, young male deer killed them by rubbing their antlers against the branches until the tree seedlings were reduced to sticks. I gave up on fruit trees and planted blueberry and raspberry bushes. Successful local orchardists construct cages around their seedlings, but mice often find them cozy places to build nests and in the process chew the roots and sometimes kill the tree.

The final part of spring lasts from early to late May when all snow is melted, but frost may still endanger young plants even as late as the first week of June. Dogwood and forsythia bloom, and apple blossoms open. Cottonwood, oaks, and maples come into full leaf. Violets create an impressionistic carpet of purple among the green grass in the field and lawn. Dandelions add the color of the sun to the lawn—indicators of healthy turf and one of the favorite foods of honeybees and bumblebees. Bluebells and trillium bloom in shadier places. Mulberry and locust leaves open toward the end of the month, and purple and white wild phlox grow luxuriously over banks and fence lines. Mayapples appear on the forest floor and bluets form a pale carpet that looks like snow.

Planting continues from mid- or late May until the end of June. The first vegetables to furnish our table are the tender asparagus tips that begin ripening in April and last until late July. A perennial, asparagus grows as high as six feet and matures over several years, each succeeding season producing more than the last. Besides the quality of soil, it is water that most determines success: abundant rainfall makes irrigation unnecessary, and if only three days pass without rain, people begin to talk about dry spells. Clarke, who comes from California, finds the most eccentric trait of Ohioans to be their definition of drought: two weeks without rain.

Last year's spinach wakes up from dormancy about the third week of April and grows until the earliest of the new spinach arrives in late June when I plow last year's under. I plant spinach three times during the summer, so we enjoy it from April until November. Rhubarb ripens the first week of May and must be used immediately as it does not freeze well, so I make stewed rhubarb and cobbler. Peas planted in early May can be harvested by late June. I plant beans and corn three times as well, two weeks apart, and harvest from July through October. Rhubarb and spinach are the easiest plants to grow, weed, and harvest. Asparagus is easy to grow and harvest but difficult to weed because I cannot cultivate around the roots; blueberries and raspberries are easy to weed and harvest but difficult to grow; strawberries are easy to grow but difficult to harvest and weed. Some rows I devote to flowers, usually marigolds and zinnias, in order to reward bees and attract butterflies but also to lure away insects that would otherwise attack the vegetables. The technique works. Ideally, every other row would be planted with flowers.

The best defense against insect damage, I have found, is not chemicals but crop rotation. Strawberries, tomatoes, peppers, and eggplant are "deep feeders" that should be rotated with nitrogen-fixing plants like peas and beans. After a strawberry crop is exhausted, in about four years, the same ground can be planted in "shallow feeders" for three to four years. Potatoes leave pathogens in the soil that attack these same varieties and must also be rotated. Legumes planted in different rows from the previous year produce more abundantly because the insects that feed on them do not seem to find the new rows. My yield more than doubled when I began rotating scientifically. A garden diary reminds me what I have planted in each row and which varieties produced the best. Still, what works one year may not work the next.

Pulling weeds can be a chore or an exercise in natural history. The term "weed" is a cultural construction referring to any plant that someone does not want. Common plantain, called English-man's foot by Native Americans, was one of nine sacred herbs of the Anglo-Saxons; Chaucer and Shakespeare cite its medicinal properties. From this auspicious beginning, the immigrant has become a weed. As well as plantain I pull curly dock, sow thistle, knotweed, white campion, creeping buttercup, common mallow, horse nettle, mullein, and sow thistle from the vegetable rows. Instead of using herbicides I control weeds in my riding arena and gravel driveway with a mixture of cider vinegar and yucca. Corn gluten can also be used to control weeds, but it has to be spread repeatedly and loses its effectiveness if applied too soon before rain. Some combinations of fatty acids can be effective, but they have to be reapplied frequently.

Summer officially begins with the solstice, but summer in northern Ohio really begins around the first or second week of June. Strawberries ripen throughout the month, although in productive years I have had strawberries from late May until mid-July. My father taught me how to grow them, planting as early as possible in April and plucking the first flowers in order to ensure a larger harvest in later years. Weeding any perennial is challenging as the root systems create channels that undesirable plants follow, primarily dandelion, thistle, and common mallow. Usually the third year yields the largest crop. Sweet or tangy depending on the variety, and picked and eaten fresh, they taste as if the sun shines from inside them.

The best time of day is just before and during sunrise. I agree with Thoreau that "morning brings back the heroic ages." Just before dawn the birds break the night silence. The eastern sky above the hills brightens before it becomes rosy and golden. Finally the sun reveals itself in the upper branches of the trees. It is over in moments, but the promise of the day is not.

Spring and early summer provide some of the most spectacular weather, sixty to seventy degrees (F). Changing light throughout the day transforms the eastern and southern hills, which are more blue or green depending on the season and cloud cover. I feel as if I live in several landscapes at once: summer light dazzles; storm clouds cast smoky gray shadows. In mornings the eastern hills are outlined in coral. Gray-green pines step from mist in a *bas relief* of trees and bushes. Silvery cold dew on fields shimmers in the muted half-light more lustrous than the fire of noontime. Dew hangs jewel-like on the orb weavers' polygonal threads strung between fence rails and stems of Queen Anne's lace. Contoured fields across the creek are all different greens— soybeans darkest, then corn, then hay and grass. Wooded hills rise above them. This luminous moment is what the inspired life is all about: filling in groundhog holes or cutting weeds can be beautiful because of the colors and the wind. Soul is that which rejoices in the life of the body.

Fog as well as light transforms landscape: on fair spring days the veil drops away to reveal the familiar trees and hills like a promise of continuance. Lifting from a stream, from the pond, or between hillside trees, fog has its own life, especially in autumn, like sea smoke rising from shoreline crags. Clouds also change the landscape. Coral light from a few strata in the east make deep green grass even greener. I love the enormous sun-filled canyons of cumulus that deepen the sky, usually in spring and summer, the curled wisps of cirrus called mare's tails, the stratocumulus that look like rolling surf, and smaller rounded clouds moving quickly like fleets of ships eastward. Seldom in Ohio is there a clear sky. I enjoy cloud-contours and regret not having become a meteorologist. Storms build up like dramatic performances. One afternoon the clouds turned a dark steel blue until the hills to the northeast took on an aspect I'd never seen before: they no longer seemed to form on the horizon but to be islands in a great body of water. The grass turned darker green. All day big cumulus built up, gold-lined. Then around 7:30 P.M. the thunderstorm began.

In late June of the year Grayfell was born, a storm blew in with gale-force winds until the smaller cedar trees bent nearly double. Several limbs came down from the Norway spruces and the elms. Rain pelted windows. We lost electricity as usual during violent weather, and the house was so quiet that I realized how much noise the water pump and refrigerator make, and I wished for a hand pump and fireplace. Even the lights give off a constant although nearly inaudible hum that I never noticed before. It was over in a half hour and clouds became mysterious convolutions like rounded hills and valleys, white and beautiful against a cobalt sky. A partial rainbow appeared. Perhaps two to three times a year I see rainbows, often full bows that reach all the way to the ground east of our house, most accompanied by shadow bows. In order to create a bow, the droplets must be round rather than oval and the sun near the opposite horizon. Bows in the eastern sky appear in the evening, while those rarer ones in the western sky appear in the morning.

Several times each summer I embark on a mission to root out wild cherry seedlings as their leaves represent an omnipresent threat to horses. Before I knew this I never noticed these trees with their beautiful, tapered green leaves and rich, coffee-colored bark. Now I have learned to spot them even among lush vegetation. Eating just one dried wild cherry leaf can poison a horse, so the owner has to clear all these trees from pasture and farm. The resilient roots, however, can travel underground. It's common to find this Hydra growing many meters from the place where I first pulled it out. It sequesters itself among thorny, invasive multiflora rose. Wild cherry has moved up and down both banks of the creek that crosses my pasture, established itself on a steep hillside, and even popped up around the house.

Clearing the fence line is one of the most difficult jobs on the place. Using a scythe, I cut away grass, thorns, and seedling trees that grow up along the wire where the mower does not reach. Tearing out wild clematis and woodbine is not difficult, but I regret having to cut down apple and honey locust seedlings, and once a well-established young white oak. If I did not clear the fence line, however, the vines would pull it down. Many trees that now act as windbreaks grew up along neglected fence lines, and for that reason in Ohio one often finds strands of old rusted wire tangled among leaves.

Like Wendell Berry in "A Good Scythe," I agree that using a scythe is easier than using a power tool for the reason that the scythe cuts a much wider swath and can be used on tall weeds with tough stems. It takes a good deal of strength and energy to use one; even with proper technique, swinging that blade requires as much exertion as climbing a long, steep incline. While I work, however, I can listen to the song of birds and hear the grasses being cut like the sound of tearing silk. Cutting with a scythe uses my own energy, and I go home tired in a good way. The power weed-eater not only destroys the peace and drowns out birdsong with its piercing noise; it also uses fossil fuel, not my own energy. While it is heavy and difficult to control, it requires the use of only a few muscles so that at the end of the day, although I am tired, I have expended no energy and am not strengthened by the work. Finally, the power tool cannot cut the heavy weeds that grow along the fence, such as wild carrot and multiflora rose, and the area it does cut is very small. When we work with our hands and arms we learn the limits of our own strength, appreciate the work done by others, and understand what is involved in taking care of the land. The work is hard, sweaty, and often frustrating, but fulfilling when I survey the cleared fence line.

Even around the flower garden I prefer to use clippers rather than a power weed eater. I find I am no more tired using the hand tool, and it takes no more time. The same is true of leaf blowers and snow blowers: the work is not easier, and noise renders it less satisfying. Power tools are complicated and costly to maintain, while the scythe has only a nut and bolt which I remove when I want to have the blade sharpened. I do not have to change oil or air and fuel filters. The only advantage of the power tool is that it gives a more finished look.

When I cut weeds along the fence line I learn to know Queen Anne's Lace, wild carrot, bull thistle, ragweed, nut sedge, phlox, blackberry, bluestem, wild oats, and brome. I identify oak, locust, cottonwood, and wild apple seedlings and hear the distinctive notes of meadow lark, chipping sparrow, wood warbler, chickadee, and bobolink. When Canada geese fly over I can stop my work and listen to the dramatic sound of their honking or their wings like cloth being shaken out. At intervals I rest and look up to survey the green hills and changing clouds.

Taking my scythe to be sharpened, however, used to involve the inevitable lecture about how much more "efficient" the power tool was. I listened because the handyman was old (I might have assumed that someone in his eighties would value tradition more, but he made his living selling these things) and then explained that gas-driven weed-eaters were too heavy for me. That was the one argument he appreciated until he ordered a line of lighter weed-eaters built to be used by women. After he died, his son, who took over the shop, dispensed with the lectures.

I kept my first scythe about fifteen years before it broke on unusually thick wild carrot, and when I looked for a new one I found I could not get one manufactured in the United States. The Chinese-made tool I bought has bolts that cannot be replaced here. The global economy found a way to punish me at last.

Summer solstice marks the shortening of days, yet the bulk of the season is still before us. Goldenrod, purple ironweed, Shasta daisy, and ox-eye daisy bloom. Hillsides where I planted crown vetch are covered in a lavender blanket. Robert Frost writes pessimistically in "The Oven Bird" that summer is a "diminished thing" because the spring flowers are so much more beautiful than those that bloom later. Certainly it is a changed thing, the dogwood, forsythia, bluebells, and violets having faded and the lime green of the grass become darker green under summer's universal fire. I don't think, however, we could endure year-round the frenzied growing and blooming of the spring any more than we could endure eternal youth. The summer has its own, subtler beauty with its longer days and early dawns. In mid-July the cicadas begin to sing, telling me the autumn will come and days are precious.

Henry David Thoreau regarded owning a farm as slavery, and some environmentalists believe that agriculture destroyed nature by harnessing it and allowing the human population to swell beyond the number the biosphere could support. On the other hand, the greatest environmentalist in American history, Aldo Leopold, writes that the danger in not owning a farm lies in thinking that food comes from the grocery store and heat from the furnace. I agree with Leopold: too many people have no idea what is involved in their survival. They take food for granted and discount the importance as well as the intelligence of farmers. At the Ohio Food and Farm Association Conference one year I learned of experts who estimate that fully half the food grown in the United States is wasted, and I wonder how sane a society can be if that is the case. The same conclusion applies to energy: we could cut nearly half our consumption with simple conservation methods such as recycling, powering down computers and turning off lights when not in use, and setting thermostats only a few degrees higher on air conditioners and lower on furnaces. Carrying our own containers, buying in bulk, and returning to the old system of requiring deposits for glass and plastic receptacles would reduce prices and cut down on litter and trash.

Thoreau lamented that he was not as wise as the day he was born, and since he was a wise man I read this passage as a wist-

ful lament that human beings tend to lose their instinctive natures as they become part of society. Aldo Leopold asserted that
education is the process of learning to see only one thing while
going blind to another, and since he was an educator, I suspect
that what he means is that with specialization we tend to lose
the sense of the wholeness of things. Each new observation or
discovery does not crowd out something else but instead widens and deepens appreciation. When I first began hiking, I saw
forests as mazes of upright trunks and tangled undergrowth.
Now I notice the sinewy bark of muscle wood, ridged bark of
the white oak, speckled bark of the wild cherry; I may spot a
trillium beside a rock in spring; I can distinguish between the
calls of ovenbird and pine warbler; I know that, when I climb a
steep trail through woods, the farther the light extends toward
the base of the tree trunks, the closer I am to the summit. Education reveals intellectual, aesthetic, and moral choices, but
learning widens and deepens perception.

Shopping for groceries is an unpleasant chore that reminds me
of how much knowledge we have lost about sustainability. Even
buying seeds and plants can be discouraging. When I first moved
here I bought starts at a small place where the knowledgeable
owner answered questions and made suggestions about different
varieties of tomatoes, peppers, and corn; nevertheless, her shop
went out of business, while the one next door, where the owner
did not know anything about crops or seeds and specialized in
lawn ornaments more than plants, stayed in business. I then located a store in Ashland where the matter-of-fact owner knew
about his products and provided different varieties of broccoli,
strawberries, and corn but shared what he knew only in a very
gruff, unfriendly manner. That person sold out to someone
who may as well have been selling plumbing supplies. Another
grower outside Ashland, with over thirty acres of bedding plants,
provides almost no choice among varieties and has so few staff

that no one has time to answer a question. Finally I located a family-run garden store south of Loudonville surrounded by fields, woods, and farms and containing two duck ponds and a garden where the bottomland was so rich the soil glistens black like coal. The building is attractive with extensive greenhouses, indoor and outdoor displays, and fruit and vegetables. Even here the people cannot tell me very much about the different plants, which varieties of tomatoes are best for canning, or anything about turf. Every year there are fewer choices of tomatoes, and usually only one variety of broccoli, peppers, melons, or squash. They do offer choices of beans and corn, but the owners cannot tell me the differences, so I have to look up the information on-line. Even on a farm and in a multigenerational family business, knowledge is not passed down. So I shop from catalogues and buy strawberries, blueberries, raspberries, and asparagus from growers out of state. Even so, from the hundreds of varieties of strawberries in the world, I may choose from about ten. Neither the global economy nor capitalism has given us greater choice.

Similarly, shopping for fruit in grocery stores is an exercise in unimaginative consumerism. Of the hundreds or so varieties of apples in the world, I never find more than eight or ten in even the largest grocery stores. There is usually little choice of any other fruit or vegetables. All the offerings are geared toward sameness except cereal where the manufacturers seem to vie to create the unhealthiest combination of sugar and salt. In markets in France, on the other hand, people can choose from a hundred kinds of cheese, while here we are lucky to find six.

In 1998 I attended a conference of the Association for the Study of Literature and Environment in Missoula. Before the conference I camped and hiked in Glacier National Park near the Canadian border. It is the most beautiful of the national parks that I've seen—Acadia, Great Smokey Mountains, Grand Tetons, Yellowstone, Olympic, Rocky Mountain, Yosemite, Giant Redwood,

Mount Rainier, Glacier Bay. The Rockies in Montana are not as high as those in Colorado, but they are bigger. I climbed Mount Brown and Grinnell Peak and hiked a trail to a pass called The Saddle where I looked over a vista that rivals anything I saw in Alaska or the Himalaya—blue-gray mountains and white glaciers that stretched to the horizon. After sitting for hours on a rock looking out over those still peaks, I hiked back and saw, far down the mountainside, a brown bear fishing in a stream that meandered through a grove of locust saplings, my first sighting of the great beings who should own this land. Years later I was able to glimpse grizzly cubs in the Grand Tetons and a pair of mating grizzlies on an island in Glacier Bay National Park.

Must we be assured of survival before we love wilderness? People did not begin to admire landscape until most could be confident of escaping starvation and until the middle class had leisure and relatively safe conveyance over distances, nor did we venerate wilderness until it had been relegated to reserves. Yet there have always been explorers, and some people have always loved to leave civilization and go to the wild places, and the desire to simplify is as old as civilization itself. Irish monks in the sixth century who desired seclusion went to the Skellig Islands in the far west and built stone huts high on the sheer cliffs. When their community grew larger in spite of the hardship of living on a nearly inaccessible rocky island, a few members moved to an even more remote part of the island to escape their like-minded brothers. Something inherent in the human psyche yearns for simplicity and for a natural environment unchanged by human habitation.

I know autumn is here when there is no manure in the barn because the horses stay out all day and all night. Some evenings the golden sunset walks across the eastern hills. Then in the west the cloud blanket turns rose and gray, like the glow of a volcano, before the dusk descends. Autumn as well as spring has three phases defined by the changing colors of leaves. For about one month, from late August until late September, the sugar maples begin to turn yellow and red while most trees are still green. Days are warm. Clarke says the pleasantest day of the year is usually September 18. The frenzy of growth is over and crops come to fruition—tomatoes, peppers, cantaloupe, beans, corn. Broccoli matures in late July, while peppers and tomatoes ripen in August and last until the first frost of October. We have tacos and salads made almost entirely of garden produce. Broccoli can be harvested until September, but we find the late broccoli to be rather bitter, so instead of eating them we allow the later heads to blossom into a mass of yellow flowerets that hum with bees, who also love the asparagus flowers. Beans grown overly ripe can be harvested for seed.

The second phase of autumn, from late September to late October, is most spectacular with red and mountain maples, flowering dogwood, black tupelo, scarlet oak, northern red oak, and pin oak turning crimson and burning bushes blazing fuchsia. Black maple, striped maple, and yellow buckeye turn golden. Sugar maple and sassafras leaves become both red and yellow. The most magnificent is the sweet gum that bears both colors at the same time. White oak attains a bronze color while Shumard oak leaves turn auburn. The peak of the colors happens usually around the third week of October. Typically the first frost occurs on October 17 with really hard frosts around the morning of the change to standard time. Green alfalfa fields alternate in contours with brown bands of harvested soybeans and swaths of yellow corn stalks still standing like stalwarts unwilling to give up. Fields are yellow with goldenrod and purple with ironweed.

The third phase lasts from late October until Thanksgiving and is characterized by different shades of bronze, auburn, and muted gold. Oak and birch hold their leaves longest while cottonwood and dogwood drop theirs earliest. We do not rake leaves but mow them with the tractor so that the blades chop the leaves into fine, shredded compost. The holiday break allows an opportunity to trim the bushes back and burn the sticks. I rototill the garden one last time, lay straw on the strawberry plants to protect them from severe winter temperatures, and cut down the cornstalks.

The process of growing with all its wayward meanderings is also the process of fruition. We reach ripeness not by making every correct choice but by error as well, because our mistakes teach us more than happening on the lucky "right" choices. The wanderings and wrong turns make people interesting. What we are left with in the end—careers that take us in unexpected directions, success or disappointment in love, places we have lived in and become part of, opportunities we passed up that haunt our memories—is what brings us to self-understanding.

Cold weather invigorates and inspires the feeling that something is about to happen. The earth is not dead: it sleeps, waiting for spring. Trees sparkle with delicate buds of frost that have grown along the branches and twigs. Winter solstice, the darkest of the year markers, also foretells the time of greatest hope. December 22 should be New Year's Day since it marks the beginning of the return of the sun.

Weather in northeastern Ohio is strongly affected by the lake, and although we do not experience the blizzards known to East Cleveland and Ashtabula, during several years when snow fell five and six feet we had to hire a farmer to plow our driveway with a backhoe. I can gauge the cold from the horses' water buckets. If they have a thin layer of ice, it is comfortable to work outside. If I have to break the ice with an ax, it is well below freezing. (I derive a peculiar pleasure from taking an ax to an iced-over water bucket.) If the buckets contain several inches of ice, it is near or below zero, and I have to bring them into the house to thaw. When the ice no longer sticks to the side of the bucket, I pitch it onto the lawn and by spring have an ice sculpture.

In January and February, snow blows and drifts, accentuating the blue of spruce branches. Snowflakes shine in wind that sculpts wells around the conifers. The wooded hills to the east are veiled gray and white. When temperatures drop into single digits and below zero, air turns blue, like crystal ice, and tree branches are encased in shimmering glass. The hills look like a Japanese ink or charcoal drawing. You can see into the very heart of the land—the snowy floor of the woods. Trees are smoky gray, black, or slate-blue in the distance with some green of hemlock.

Winter colors can dazzle as spectacularly as those of other seasons because of the stark contrast. The stems of dead Queen Anne's lace and other plants turn auburn red against the snow. Cardinals blaze russet. Corn stalks and leaves not cut down look golden brown against the white. When snow falls or is blown on wind, all is lace. Dawn casts diamond pinpoints of blue, green, yellow, orange, red, purple, and silver on the undulating white blanket.

One January Colleen and I found a dead mole lying on bloody snow, a series of straight lines fanned out around it. This rune, probably impressed into the snow by the beating wings of a hawk or owl scared away before finishing his meal, conveys the message of the wild, that all creatures must live their own natures, that some must die in order to ensure survival for others.

Winter provides the best time for writing and reflection, for testing oneself against the weather, for learning to live within the limits the earth imposes. Snow makes me appreciate the coziness of the house, but it also makes me feel as if every time I leave the house I embark on an adventure. I like walking in falling snow and seeing the pure-white folds and cornices sculpted by wind. Winter brings us to our senses, the thrill of the cold wind teaching us that we live at the mercy of the earth that forms us. Storms also remind us that we do not own the earth; it owns us, and we mistreat it to our peril. The winter of 2014 brought record-breaking cold temperatures, sometimes as low as minus twenty degrees. The water pipe that ran from the house to the barn was frozen for six weeks, and I transported the horses' water in milk jugs on a sled. That season provided my first experience of snow rollers, hollow tubes of snow created by wind. This rare and wonderful phenomenon occurs when sunlight causes the surface layer to begin thawing over a substrate of ice or powder to which the upper layer will not adhere; wind blows the exposed snow, but its weight prevents it from traveling far. Instead, the snow layer curls into cylinders that look as if they are created by people or animals, but there are no footprints or hoof marks around them. Absent the scientific explanation, people might have speculated that snow rollers are the work of fairies or other winged creatures.

At last, March brings the equinox and snow squalls turn the air to lace followed by bright spells and snow melting on green swaths of grass. Of all months, March is the least predictable with the largest variation among temperatures. Ice is a greater problem then than in January; the most hazardous kind, called "black ice," forms on pavement. Always, there is at least one large snowstorm in late March that blows in suddenly and, usually, just as suddenly melts. Rivers and creeks rise, sometimes dramatically. One year the little stream in our pasture flooded so extensively that it carved out new banks even though the thick vegetation should have held the soil. I had to reset the fence post on the north side, since the ground around it had been washed away to bedrock, and the post itself hung in mid-air, held up only by wire.

As I change the oil in the tractor to get it ready for spring I think about necessary work versus drudgery. Drudgery means labor for unfairly low wages that enriches the employer while impoverishing the worker. Good labor not only benefits the worker but allows her to realize some accomplishment. We should enjoy putting in the effort to live on the earth, as Wendell Berry argues in "Home of the Free." Especially in this age of specialization we should know what goes into the other tasks that support ours. Because one job requires less training or skill than another does not diminish its value. No work should be deprecated except shoddy work. The bank janitor and clerk are as important as the president, venture capitalist, or investor, and their actions not likely to create massive recession.

❧

Clarke asked me what famous person I would choose to be if I could. Certainly not my hero, Mary Wollstonecraft Godwin, whose personal sacrifice transformed the lives of women after her but whose own life was difficult and short. I admire fearlessness (as distinguished from heroism, bravery, or courage) and even a certain amount of recklessness if it is inspired by curiosity or love of the natural world. If I could choose another life it would be that of Friederike Victoria "Joy" Adamson, an Austrian woman who immigrated to Kenya in the 1940s to escape Hitler's Anschluss and worked there with lions and cheetahs. She lived several lives at once: as a biologist, she helped to restore animal habitat and returned orphaned lions and cheetahs to the wild; as an artist, she painted wildflowers that had never before been recorded; as a writer, she preserved the story of her work, most famously in *Born Free*; as a conservationist, she traveled the world educating people about the importance of preserving the megafauna found nowhere else. Two marriages ended in divorce, but her third husband, British zoologist George Adamson, possessed the same lust for life that Joy had and, like her, stayed active into late age. They died for higher causes: both were murdered, Joy by one of her own employees and George by poachers who were trying to kill a tourist.

Ever since I read *Our Town* in high school, I knew I wanted to live an active life. In act 3, Emily Webb asks whether anyone ever really understands the importance of being alive. The stage manager–chorus answers, "The poets and saints do, maybe, some." I used to wonder whether it was possible to live the active life in the modern world with its automation and information economy. Work should be done purposefully and carefully, but the worker should also know why it must be done, how tasks were accomplished by those who came before, and how one's own work contributes to that of others. I am speaking of art and labor both, of painting pictures or writing poems, but also of plowing, harvesting, clearing fence lines, or mowing grass.

The active life involves more than physical work and is not merely "busy." Activity must be done well but also mindfully, with the inspiration of a quest. Wendell Berry writes that plowing with horses is a "song." A verse from the Upanishads states that "Prayer is perfect when he who prays, remembers not that he is praying." The Maitri Upanishad further advises the reader to "keep the mind pure, for what a man thinks, that he becomes." Walter Pater wrote that all life must become ritual. W. B. Yeats finishes "Among School Children" with the question "How can we know the dancer from the dance?" When I work, I am both what I do and what I think about while I work. Human bodies were built to walk, not to sit. In order to live a full life we must use arms, legs, and hands as much as we can, yet the mind must also be engaged. When I move a pile of composted manure from the paddock to the garden, I think not of drudgery but usefulness. When I am tired, I remind myself that doing hard, dirty work is better than not being able to do it. Negative thoughts defile the purity of action.

A person can live the active life in the city as well as in the country, but she cannot live actively if she ignores the earth.

In February every year at the annual convention of the Ohio Ecological Food and Farm Association (OEFFA), keynote speakers talk about such subjects as conservation, encroachment by the oil and gas industry, saving family farms, ways of financing small farms, and combating the influence of agribusiness and chemical companies like Monsanto, which has created seeds genetically modified to withstand spraying by the herbicide glyphosate, also developed by Monsanto and detected in the food chain and even in mothers' milk. Seminar leaders advise attendees in the best ways to grow blueberries and brambles, raise apple trees, rotate crops, install solar panels, control weeds naturally, prevent soil erosion, and defend communities against horizontal hydraulic fracturing. Spending two days among more than a thousand people interested in organic farming and gardening inspires me for a new year of planting and harvesting and makes me wish I had majored in agronomy.

Farm tours sponsored by OEFFA demonstrate the success of organic farming: a farmer in northern Ashland County uses partial tillage—leaving large clods of earth in rows between crops—to control weeds; crushed walnut shells also inhibit weeds along fence lines; a young husband and wife in Knox County run an egg, turkey, pork, and dairy operation in which the animals (including the hens) graze in a succession of "cells," areas of a larger pasture cordoned off by movable electric wire. Cattle are rotated several times a day in order to keep them from overgrazing any one area; as they eat the tops of the grass, their hooves press the lower stalk into the earth where it decomposes into more fertile soil. This method of rotation, the farmer claims, fixes one hundred pounds of nitrogen per acre per year. Hens in movable wire pens follow, and their instinctive scratching through cattle dung separates and aerates it for further decomposition of organic matter. Turkeys also graze freely in rotated pastures, protected from nocturnal predators by a pair of vigilant geese who will take on foxes, dogs, and even coyotes. Pigs forage beneath a tree line that separates the organic farm from a neighbor whose farm is not certified organic (the "buffer zone" must be twenty-five feet), feeding on their favorite food—acorns—and other plants as they trample weeds. Because of continuous rotation of different animals, the pastures never need mowing, reseeding, or fertilizing. Swarms of flies, which create problems for neighbors of feed-lot farms, are unknown since the manure is composted into soil; the flies that land on the cattle are eaten by cowbirds that live in the woods surrounding the fields. Our neighbors across Honey Creek (husband, wife, and three daughters) rotate organic beef cattle and chickens on this principle of cell grazing. They keep a goat for milk and butter and grow all their own vegetables and fruit.

I walked the township road that crosses Honey Creek and ascends the hill to the east and noted the brambles and seedling trees rising from last year's fallen leaves and competing with each other for the available water and space. Human beings have been created no more purposefully than a tree that manages to take root in the woods, started from a seed dropped by a bird or squirrel. Perhaps we should see ourselves, no less than any tree, as part of a thriving ecosystem, offspring of the land. How can this whole intricate ecosystem and the spirit that animates it care only about human beings? The divine is not the individual bee but the instinct of the bee covering its legs with pollen; not the horse but the speed of the horse pounding thunder out of the ground; not the flower but what propels it open in the spring.

For millennia the earth has been displaying its intelligence in old-growth forests. We need to recover that intelligence lost with the invention of plow, sword, and wheel. Our fall was not in rebellion but in learning to fear the world and not feel at home in it. Daily, we should practice the art of belonging and living—not as if each day were the last, as the saying has it, but as if it were the first, a door opening, not a door closing. Health is the health of all ecosystems; a farm should resemble as much as possible a natural ecosystem, and we should be directly related to the sources of life. Even the history of our language tells us this, as tree names are some of the oldest Anglo-Saxon words. The earth is more than four billion years old. Upright-walking australopithecine creatures appeared only about three million years ago, *Homo sapiens* has been around for only about 315,000 years, and agriculture that enabled civilization to evolve is only 10,000 years old. We are newcomers who need to respect the inhabitants who have been here so long before us; we are caretakers, not owners, of this garden, and we need only look around to see that nature is trying to show us the gate that will lead us back inside.

Chapter Six

Inhabitants

WHAT MAKES ME think I own this place? Not only have many people occupied the house and worked the farm before me, but many of its current inhabitants pay me less heed than I give to ants or houseflies (who actually command much of my attention). I speak not only of the songbirds, woodpeckers, and hummingbirds I try to attract with my feeders and birdhouses but also of the uninvited guests who find my place amenable to their needs. There is no particular reason they should not regard it as theirs rather than mine. We invade their homes and they make use of ours, living here regardless of what we think or do.

Robin Wall Kimmerer in *Braiding Sweetgrass* explains the belief of the native people of the Great Lakes that, contrary to the idea that *Homo sapiens* is the pinnacle of evolution, human beings are at the bottom, the most recent with the most to learn, and the best teachers are the plants and animals whose wisdom is apparent in that they know instinctively how to live. Seeds and roots contain all the information that plants need in order to survive, and animals learn quickly from mothers or family groups. We, on the other hand, take eighteen years to mature, and even then, most of us could not survive on our own. We are also the only creatures foolish enough to destroy our own habitat.

While I have always been an observer of birds and wildflowers, it was Colleen who taught me most about perception. We walked many times throughout the day but always at dusk, when we circled the lawn, checking on the horses and hens, Soxie the cat accompanying us. Although I have owned more than twenty-five cats and seven horses, I have called only two dogs my own: a mixed-breed beagle with a broken tail named Duke who was my companion throughout high school, and Colleen, whose long, black-and-buff-colored hair and curving tail gave evidence that she was partly Norwegian elkhound and partly something else— we never knew what. As she ran about the lawn and smelled the grass and air, she showed me that I know almost nothing about the creatures that live and visit here. Each area of a stem of grass carried for her a code revealing what transpired not only during the night but also days and perhaps even weeks earlier. She loved the outside: in winter she scooped up snow the way a pelican scoops fish and caught large falling flakes on her tongue. Perhaps some ancient instinct was at work here. In summer she rolled in the grass and ran great circles around the lawn, a constant presence for fourteen years. Thirteen years after she died, we still miss her and talk about her.

We acquired her when her previous owner, who owned too many dogs for the space available, advertised her as a one-year-old Border collie (she was not) who loved people and needed a good home. Most dogs love people who do not mistreat or neglect them. Colleen adored us. She turned Clarke into a dog person and then an animal person. Her expressive eyes and mute adoration overcame his reluctance to have an animal in the house, owing to a childhood spent without pets. Her sensitive ears were always tuned to the words she liked best—*go, out, walk*. She understood more about us than we ever did about her, master as she was of human nonverbal communication. Tying the strings on my hiking boots meant to her that we were headed for the Mohican Park. When I pulled on Wellington boots she knew we would go out to do chores. She knew which clothes I wore for teaching (when I put them on she became visibly depressed) and which I put on for work around the place.

Colleen had one flaw—her dislike of cats. Although she never tried to injure any, she disdained them, especially when I paid them attention. She lived in perpetual disappointment, however, because a farm will never be without cats. People drop them off when we are not at home and even when we are. Resentful at first, I learned over the years to value the abandoned ones especially and now think of the people who leave them as anonymous donors. Socks Van Gogh, whom we called Soxie, was a tabby with a white bib and boots. The surname originated when she lost the tip of her right ear in a fight. Her enormous green eyes were proportionally even larger than most cats', and, although slightly bowlegged, she was slender and beautiful. She carried her tail straight up. Although I was unable to lay a hand on her for six months, she became one of my favorites—an excellent mouser who walked with Colleen and me in the evenings. Shy but affectionate, she lived the most fulfilled life on the farm: her work was her play; her time was her own. When she wanted to come inside she clung to the screen door until we let her in; she was at home sleeping on our bed or in the barn.

Soxie came to us the first year we lived here. Several years later, two gray and white kittens came running to me out of the evening fog. We named them Hansel and Gretel. I eventually found a home for Gretel, and to this day I regret adopting her out as I was more attached to her than I thought. We nicknamed her brother Bardolph because he had a bright pink nose like the character in the *Henry IV* plays, although he was a good deal wiser, and it was to that name he answered. He carried his tail curved like a question mark as if he were asking the meaning of all he surveyed. While he understood me immediately, it took me four years to realize his value. He came when called like a dog, accompanied Colleen and me on walks, stayed away from the road, and never voluntarily left the property. Other cats never hissed at him, even at first meeting; not once did he get into a fight. On the contrary, he served as peacemaker, caretaker of kittens, official welcomer of new arrivals. A feline *bodhisattva*, he seemed to embrace the philosophy that sharing meant there would be enough for all. Most distinctively, he vocalized when I spoke his name and when I held him placed his paw gently on my face. He lived to be nearly fifteen when his hind legs, crippled with arthritis, collapsed beneath him, and we reluctantly put him down.

Bardolph died in August 2012; in November of that year another cat, a yellow tiger, appeared at the front door begging for food. I took him in with the intention of neutering him and taking him to the local feline adoption agency, as six cats lived here already, but he had other plans and established himself immediately as a favorite. Clarke wanted to name him Lefty because his head tilted slightly left; I wanted to call him Pumpkin for his color, so we called him Lefty/Pumpkin. He was the most demonstrably affectionate barn cat I have ever owned, begging to be picked up each time he saw me and rubbing his head against my neck. He loved life: always he played, climbed, jumped, ran, explored. On April 2, 2014, he did not show up for the morning feeding, and a few days later we found him in a tuft of grass, his neck broken by dogs that had been running loose at night. We still feel the void created by his passing.

Horses, usually suspicious of dogs, liked Colleen. They love cats, however. I have seen horses scratching a cat's head gently with their soft noses. They will rub a cat's belly, allow a cat to sleep on their backs, and nibble carefully around one sleeping in their hay. Dakota stroked the ears of one of my barn cats, Guy Noir (he was black), with his large lips; I have seen them greeting each other by touching noses. Once I saw Xanadu step gingerly over Bardolph, lying in the doorway of the barn, rather than disturb him.

When we first moved to Ashland County I kept six New Hampshire red hens in a shed with a fenced run. I didn't let them forage freely because I had sighted red foxes several times; coyotes had moved eastward, and I often heard them barking in the evening. I named the older hens for the goddesses Hera,

Minerva (the feistiest hen), and Ceres while the younger were Pertelote, Partlett, and Guinevere. They usually produced six large eggs a day—more than we used, so I sold them at a local farm market. In the evening just before they roosted I fed them corn out of my hand. They came to me when I entered their pen and even lost their fear of Colleen. Five died of old age, while Partlett was taken by a fox which slipped through a hole in the wire I thought too small to admit a predator. The next morning, nothing was left but a pile of soft, red feathers.

Largest and most prominent of the wild inhabitants are the white-tailed deer, which prosper in the absence of their greatest predators, the mountain lion and timber wolf. When Clarke and I first moved here, Colleen was young, and although she slept in the house, her smell was everywhere outside, so the deer stayed toward the back of the property where they killed my cherry trees and sampled the garden produce. As Colleen grew older, they gradually moved closer to the house, and after she died they made the entire lawn their nighttime playground. Especially in the fall during rut, I find their hoof marks on the sand of my riding arena and torn-up turf on the lawn where they have been sporting. I see their two-toed prints in the snow, sometimes solitary, sometimes in groups. Nearly blind by human standards, they see shapes and movement but not details and know their world through their senses of smell—more acute than a bloodhound's—and of hearing. They can turn the pinnae, or large outer ears, in three directions, an ability which helps them evade predators. Beautiful to watch browsing in a field or following each other single file along Honey Creek, and highly intelligent, they communicate with each other by wagging an ear or flipping a tail. I have seen as many as thirteen in a group and spot one or two every time I ride horses at Malabar Farm. Bird netting keeps them out of the strawberries and blueberries. For a time we kept them out of the corn with aluminum pie plates tied to fence posts that bang incessantly in the wind and a Japanese invention called flash tape—narrow strips of colorful shiny plastic which dance and shimmer like fire—but they wised up quickly and now help themselves, most years leaving us enough. Their own speed is their safety, but they become confused by the noise and lights of automobiles. Like human beings, many are killed on the road, but nevertheless their population is said to be increasing beyond sustainability.

One spring a neighbor called to tell me there was an abandoned fawn in my pasture. As I stepped across the stream, the speckled baby leaped up and trotted away and into a hillside thicket. It had not been abandoned; does leave their fawns alone during the day, when their presence would signal to predators the whereabouts of the young, and return to nurse at night. If the fawn had truly been abandoned it would have wandered about the pasture crying. After that incident, I noticed that every year a doe raises her fawn in my pasture, nearly unseen. I am careful to make sure the fawns are weaned before we mow.

One danger for horses is the pesky groundhog, also called woodchuck because of the Native American name wushak, a term that has nothing to do with wood. A large rodent, it digs holes in the earth just large enough for a horse's foot to get caught in and just deep enough for the leg to go down into. A horse going fast enough can injure a tendon or break a leg in which latter case it must usually be destroyed. Groundhogs nevertheless aerate the soil and are said to turn up six hundred thousand tons of soil per year in the United States. They make their first appearances in late March and early April. People get rid of groundhogs by poisoning, shooting, trapping, or smoking them out of their holes. The best way I know of to discourage them is to keep a dog that can harass them into moving away, but it has to be a big, aggressive dog. Colleen was neither. I simply fill in the holes as I find them, and usually the groundhogs give up and eventually migrate. I trap the more determined ones, using apples as bait (they are suckers for apples), and transport them to the Mohican Forest. (In 2017 my catch totaled six.) The groundhog ripples over the grass like a monk in flowing robes and pours itself down the hole it has laboriously excavated but sometimes turns back to look at me, perhaps calculating the threat. One stood its ground when I was riding the pony Shio on a tractor path but decided the combination of horse and rider was too much and decamped. Another stood up to Clarke when he turned into the driveway where the groundhog was busily feasting on fallen pears. Clarke interpreted his indecision as the reflexive question, "Should I get out of the way or can I take this measly Geo-Metro?" If that was what it was thinking, the woodchuck decided against the latter strategy and waddled away.

Opossums are infrequent visitors to the hayloft. I trap them and take them to the park because their feces contain a bacterium that can cause neurological disease in horses. Raccoons I leave alone. Although they dig up flowers, raid bird feeders, drink from my barn cats' water dishes, and sometimes trash some of my corn crop, they usually do not interfere with horses. They occupy vacated groundhog dens usually in heavy brush where horses cannot go, and they are interesting with their bandit faces and nocturnal comings and goings. I sometimes happen upon them if I go out to the barn after dark and they have already entered the feed room in search of cat food. They usually skitter away when they see me. Once a raccoon swung down from the hayloft, hung for a moment by an arm, and faced me like Tarzan in the lianas before it decided to dispense with introductions, leaped to the floor, and scrabbled into the shadows. Skunks wander through but never stay—fortunately, as they are the most frequent carriers of rabies of any mammal in North America. Although I have heard landowners say that coyotes will attack skunks, most predators are wise enough to avoid them.

Recently an eastern red squirrel has also taken up residence in one of my log-pile horse jumps.

Frequently I see reddish-brown eastern chipmunks with their distinctive white stripes in the woods, and several live in a crack in our concrete stoop on the north side of the house and take what the birds throw down from the feeders. I love to watch their quick, jerky little movements when they groom themselves or turn seeds or nuts around in tiny, dexterous paws. Like squirrels, they make opportune use of what we have. I put out nuts and dried fruit for them and watch while they come and go to the nearby pine windbreak. Sometimes they let me approach as close as ten feet.

The fogs of springtime accompany the earliest sounds. The first harbingers of the vernal equinox are the ascending bird-like whistles of spring peepers, seldom seen by people; later, their songs are mingled with the loud, resonating trill of gray tree frogs (they are actually green), raspy quack of wood frogs, G-string twang of green frogs, and throaty jug-o-rum from amorous bull frogs. The thunderous cacophony becomes exuberant when birds called nightjars utter their zipping sounds. Frogs and toads are great consumers of mosquitoes and other insects that feed on vegetables. Whenever I see a toad in the barn or garage I capture it and place it beneath the rhubarb leaves or asparagus ferns, hoping it will take up residence in the garden.

For several years in March, local naturalist and photographer David Fitzsimmons has shown me the place at Malabar Farm where the salamanders dance. With the help of flashlights, we find our way through heavy brush to a vernal pool—shallow snowmelt that dries up in April or May. Visible only in late evening, spotted and Jefferson salamanders swim upward from the bottom in corkscrew fashion to the surface to attract a mate. The woods are thunderous with the sound of tree frogs and spring peepers. A whole ecosystem thrives, unknown to most human beings.

The pond in my pasture is also home to painted and eastern box turtles as well as big snappers. Colleen and I found a snapping turtle, looking from a distance like a large rock, in a water-filled swale on the township road one spring day when we were out walking. It did not withdraw its head even when I touched the carapace. Colleen wanted to investigate, but I kept her away from the powerful beak. In its own good time, the turtle heaved itself out of the water, propelled itself across the road, slid down the bank, and plunged into the drainage ditch that empties into Honey Creek. With their sage expressions and long life spans, snappers seem to represent the integrity of the entire biosphere. As I walk around the edge of the pond, I hear the splash of frogs and turtles before I see them. I want to tell them I mean them no harm and will not allow trappers on the property, but they take no chances. To them I am an ominous shadow not of their kind, an intruder, and, evolutionarily speaking, a late-comer, but watching them and listening to the birds and frogs, I regret that I did not become a biologist.

Our bank barn hosts many creatures who find its rafters and corners an ideal home. Once I found a snipe nesting in the saw-dust on the barn floor. I hear the clicking and squeaking of bats whenever I go into the hayloft. They leave their guano on the floor, but they repay me for the trouble of cleaning up after them by keeping the mosquito population down. I know how trun-cated the human auditory sense is when I realize they can hear a fly cleaning its wings. Bats create colonies in rafters where they hang upside down during the day; at night I see them fluttering away from the barn roof like ships setting sail from the harbor.

One year while weeding I surprised a fox snake in the gar-den. It was reddish brown with distinctive dark blotches. Many fox snakes are killed because of mistaken identity: their coloring leads people to think they are copperheads, while their small vibrating tails cause them to be taken for rattlesnakes. Later my snake turned up in the strawberry garden. Soxie circled it curi-ously while it lay coiled, watching her intently. At last she wisely gave up, leaving the snake master of the situation. After a few weeks, the fox snake chose the garage as refuge, lying there nearly three days, curled in a dark corner. Still later, Hansel found our fox snake wrapped around the water heater in the basement; it had probably gained access through a small opening in the mor-tar of the basement storm door. Snakes belong in the garden, not in the house. With a broom, Clarke and I hustled it into a cardboard box, as snakes do not retreat from harassment but go toward it. We closed the lid with the critter inside, transported it to the hayfield, and released it. I imagine he (or she) relates this story to friends of having found the way into a castle only to have the resident giants first imprison and then release him, to joyful relief. We have not encountered any fox snakes since, and we have repaired the mortar beneath the storm door.

Each spring the red-winged blackbirds are the first to accompany me while I rake and hoe the garden soil, shrilling their three-note song and populating the cattails around my pond. Robins also fly down to feed on the earthworms I turn up. Later I have the song of the field sparrows. I hang a thistle feeder and mixed seed feeder outside one of the windows and in winter a suet holder. Year-round visitors are chipping sparrows, field sparrows, purple finches, slate-colored juncos, cardinals, goldfinches, and chickadees. In the spring I have seen brown-headed cowbirds, red-and white-breasted nuthatches, ruby-crowned kinglets, brown thrashers, house wrens, ruby-capped sparrows, titmice, vesper sparrows, black-headed grosbeaks, rose-breasted grosbeaks, evening grosbeaks, and song sparrows. Migrating pine warblers and northern mockingbirds feast on the fruit of lingonberry bushes my predecessor planted behind the house. Perhaps they view me as the African bird views the rhinoceros on whose back it rides, picking at insects on the rhino's skin: I am just another creature providing an opportunity for food.

Omnipresent from May until September when they begin their journey to Mexico, the ruby-throated hummingbirds are feisty, aggressive, and territorial. If I am not quick enough in spring to hang the feeder, they hover just outside the dining room window and sometimes even tap their beaks on the glass. Although my feeder has four stations, only one male or two females will feed at any one time. Males spar with each other in midair, emitting high-pitched squeals. At about three inches long, they are the smallest North American birds, but their quickness and agility make them fearless, and indeed I have never seen one in the jaws of a cat. One year when I climbed in Rocky Mountain National Park, a hummingbird pecked at my bright red helmet. They drink their three-ounce weight in nectar every day, and their tiny nests are woven of the smallest pieces of grass and bound with threads of spider webs. The nectar feeder is also the favorite haunt of the magnificent Baltimore oriole, which has become more frequent over the years. Their melodic song is some of the most beautiful natural music I have heard.

Frequent visitors for the first ten years we lived here were the bluebirds, who do not visit feeders. In flight they look like pieces of the sky. I kept a bluebird trail of four boxes on T-posts facing the woods to the east. At least once a week I had to open the boxes to remove the sparrow nests. House sparrows are dominant over bluebirds and will take over if they are allowed, but they can build almost anywhere, while bluebirds require a hollowed-out space. Cutting and pruning of trees has eliminated many of the holes they used to occupy. Bluebirds build small, round nests with oval centers, while sparrows construct large, rambling nests. When I saw the male bluebirds perched on the boxes in the evenings like householders sitting on their porches after a day's work, I knew they had established themselves. After 2003 they became rarer, but not because their numbers were dwindling: the efforts of birders and bluebird societies have succeeded in increasing their population, but they like open ground, and my trees had grown to such maturity in those ten years that the bluebirds moved away. I still see one or two visiting the birdbath and sitting on fence posts but have only a few sightings now each summer, whereas I used to see several every day. Once I sighted an indigo bunting, known for its brilliant azure color, in a bush outside the house. These birds are difficult to spot because they usually dwell high in the trees and from the ground appear like black silhouettes.

I allow tree swallows and house wrens to nest in bluebird boxes and often find perfectly round wrens' nests in the branches of shrubs and white pines. Once I discovered an abandoned nest in which the wren mother had woven a soft under-layer of Kestrel's chestnut-colored hair into the center. The bird had also used Shio's long black hair to bind the little twigs and stemmy grass. I could not even pull one hair from the nest, so intricately and tightly was it woven among the smallest twigs I had ever examined.

Pheasants were common in the early 1990s but not so much in later years. Others birds I saw with some frequency in the fields surrounding our place were bobwhites (whose loud song is unmistakable), eastern phoebes, and Carolina wrens. Several times I spotted yellow-shafted flickers in the long grasses near the field, and every January I saw eastern meadowlarks with their distinctive black V on sun-yellow breasts sitting on the paddock fence. When my neighbor mowed his field and fenced it in for cattle in 2008, they disappeared.

The elusive wood thrush calling from across Honey Creek makes a series of melodious phrases followed by a guttural trill. The field sparrow's song is a slurred whistle in increasing tempo. Meadowlarks make a clear, slurred whistle. One of the most memorable is the white-throated sparrow whose song is a series of flutelike phrases in increasing length, which accompanied me as I climbed Mount Katahdin in Maine and now follow me as I hike in the Mohican woods. One harsh winter a beautiful snow bunting hovered near my tractor, seeming to stand still in a very strong wind before seeking shelter on a rafter in the garage.

Regular visitors to my pond and Honey Creek include mallards, Canada geese, and great blue herons. More gray than blue, the herons fly over with their legs out behind them, necks craned in an S shape. They lift off from the water nearly vertically and will not stay if I step closer than a hundred feet. Bufflehead ducks traveling through to Canada from the south in March float on my neighbor's pond. I have spotted loons and common gallinules there. In the rushes near my own smaller pond I sometimes happen upon nesting American woodcocks. Horseback riders frequently see woodcocks because they tend to nest in brush or leaves near open spaces. The birds do not fly as I approach but utter a plaintive moan whereupon I leave them to their musings. On a few occasions, snowy egrets and great white herons have graced my pasture during their migrations in early summer, walking through high grass and feeding on grasshoppers and beetles. Sandhill cranes make their homes on low-lying fields near the Mohican River and at wetlands in various places throughout the county.

Most years a pair of Canada geese build their nest on a tuft of grass on the bank of the pond, and after the goslings hatch, the brood (usually about seven) strut in a line across the pasture with one parent leading and the other bringing up the rear. Of all the migrators I witness, Canada geese are the most abundant, adults flying in V formation northward in spring and summer, southward in fall and winter, the long ribbon of their bodies flung purposely through the air. Honking exuberantly as they trace their ancestral routes hundreds of miles, they spiral over the pond, hold their wings bell-shaped to arrest their speed upon descent, and create a wake as they splash down on the surface.

Barn and cliff swallows arrive in early or mid-May and build their half-shell or water-jug nests on the beams in the understory. Perhaps they are descendants of birds who arrived here long ago just as the human inhabitants were all descendants of immigrants. They nest all summer, the young not fledging until August or even September. They are omnipresent, shrieking every time I enter the barn, dive-bombing my barn cats, and circling me as I turn up worms and insects with my rototiller. In July and August when I mow the field they weave an aerial dance before me, catching on the wing the gnats and mosquitoes my tractor flings up. Occasionally a swallow fledgling, grown too large for the nest, falls to the barn floor or lawn, in which case I lift it back. Swallows are voluminous insect eaters and so, like the bats, repay me for cleaning up their dung. As soon as the young fledge in late summer, they disappear, abandoning the barn to eerie silence. I leave the old swallow nests affixed to the beams in the barn for returning birds who need immediate accommodations after migration. Aldo Leopold advocates knocking down these nests so that the swallows must build anew, because the old ones may contain parasites harmful to the young, but one year after I took them down too early I found four dead swallows in a bluebird box where they had huddled together for warmth. Since then I have left the nests alone.

One summer I found a sparrow fledgling in the grass not near any nest. Following instructions from the Ohio Bird Sanctuary in Mansfield, I gave it water with an eye dropper, fed it cat food softened to mush, and set it on the highest branch I could reach. Mother birds can recognize the chirping of their own chicks and will continue to feed them after they leave the nest. Handling by human beings does not deter them, for all the folklore about mother birds not returning if people interfere. In this case, the chick turned around and crawled back into my hand and up my arm. I set it back on the branch and walked away.

The year Grayfell was born, a bobolink bubbled and gurgled in the high grass along the edge of the fence as I planted. In later years bobolinks have decreased, and I have not seen one on my place for about ten years, although many are sighted at a county wildlife sanctuary a few miles to the north.

Several times I've found small pieces of cellophane in the middle of sparrow nests, and once a piece of brown cotton, a poignant reminder of the day when Colleen and I played tug-of-war on the lawn with an old brown knee sock. She snatched the toy from me and dashed off with it, leaving a small triangle of cloth lying on the grass. I ran after her, forgetting to pick up the torn piece. There it lay—small, brown, triangular—connecting me to that afternoon when I played with my dog and to the adult bird who had salvaged it to create a soft place to lay her eggs. We are all of one fabric of the world.

Because my neighbor stocks his pond with fish, eagles fly over and perch in the highest treetops. Eagle nests have been sighted a few miles away near Malabar Farm. I had seen eagles in the wild on Assateague Island, Virginia, and Glacier Bay National Park in Alaska; in Juneau I saw them as frequently as I see robins in Ohio. I rejoice that pesticides that damaged their eggshell formation and reduced their numbers have been banned but regret that we have been unable to protect the habitat of bobolink and eastern meadowlark.

Kestrels use my clothesline pole to survey the prospects of a meal. One year I saw what I thought was an injured bird fluttering in the garden and went out to learn that two kestrels were mating. Another found its way into the tack room of the barn, no doubt looking for game and unable to find its way out. As I captured it in a net for release, I was able to observe closely the blue wing feathers, speckled breast, and fierce yellow eyes. Frequently I catch and release barn swallows, sparrows, and robins that have become trapped in the feed room.

Starlings are not usually regarded as beautiful, but in midfall every year these European immigrants weave beautiful patterns above the fields, rising, swooping, and diving in undulating aerial shapes, no bird ever losing its place in the flock. They gather on the telephone wires, a great chorus raising a loud ode to time, change, and destiny; then suddenly they fly all at once, leaving the wires and treetops empty and the fields silent. After they migrate in late fall, I hang suet feeders for the downy and red-bellied woodpeckers; when starlings are in residence they congregate at suet feeders and chase woodpeckers away.

Vultures circle overhead, watching to carry to the other life whatever can no longer bear this one. Red tails and rough-legged hawks frequent the trees near the riding area. I have sighted quail on a few occasions but see wild turkeys several times a week. Once a female peregrine perched on my clothesline pole, and a few times I have been lucky enough to catch a glimpse of a northern goshawk. I am sometimes lucky enough to hear owls hooting in the morning or evening. One year I heard several screech owls in the white pines behind the house.

Sparrows flutter outside my window, sometimes with grass in their beaks, looking for a place to build. Mourning doves hover near cypresses that frame the front of the house, and a Carolina wren once perched on my windowsill, scooped up the shells of dead ladybugs, and looked at me for a long time unconcerned before departing. Sometimes I find birds that have collided with a window lying on the pavement outside the sunroom. If they are not killed, I put them into a cage so the cats cannot get to them. They recover after a few hours, when I can release them. One year a female golden-crowned kinglet hit the window and lay stunned; I put it into the cage inside the sunroom. Going to check on it, I found the door still closed but the bird gone; having worked its way out through one of the holes, it was loose in the house. When my search turned up nothing, I assumed the cats had captured and eaten it. After I returned from work, Clarke told me that when he got home he saw one of the indoor cats, the calico Bodie, sitting on the windowsill in the kitchen looking down at a bird right next to her. Clarke approached and, when the bird did not fly, raised the sash and then the screen. Neither bird nor cat moved, so he pushed the bird forward, and it spread its wings and flew.

In May 2011 on a bright day following a storm, I returned from a ride on Dakota when I saw a large white bird with charcoal wing tips strolling on the concrete dais in the middle of the lower barn. After I untacked the horse and put the saddle and equipment away, the bird was still there, looking up at me as no wild bird would do. I fed it fennel and sunflower seeds and caught it with my hands; it was banded, so I placed it inside a rabbit hutch and searched "homing pigeon" online. The first link to pop up was the American Racing Pigeon Union, and the first screen had a box into which the user could key in the band number of a found bird; hitting "enter" brought up the owner's contact information together with instructions on how to care for the bird until it could be returned. (These people are organized.) I learned that the birds' water had to be several inches deep since pigeons do not drink as other birds do but siphon water through a hole in the tops of their beaks. They should be fed cornmeal, but as I had none, I continued to feed him wild birdseed.

I left a message at the number listed for found birds, and the next day the owner called to say that one of his young breeding males was indeed lost, that it had been blown eastward by a storm when it was out for exercise. Its home was Defiance, Ohio, about 150 miles to the northwest. The man sent me a cardboard shipping carton with air holes covered with permeable gauze so the bird could breathe but not stick its head out the opening. The carton was to be shipped "priority," as all live animals have to be, since they are without water until they reach their destination. I took the bird to the post office in Loudonville where the postal clerk accepted it without surprise, stamped the carton, prepared the address, and whisked it to a back room. On the way home I felt a tremendous sadness. The beautiful pigeon had filled my days with his sweet cooing; besides, I become attached to animals I have fed and taken care of. The owner told me that the bird had probably chosen my barn because his pigeons lived in a bank barn from which the upper floor had been removed so the birds could have the whole space to fly around in. He owned about fifteen thousand dollars' worth of pigeons. The bird was not so far from home as I thought: what birders like him do is drive to Missouri and release the pigeons, who fly home, often arriving before the people. (It makes as much sense as any other sport.)

Although the human eye is able to perceive nearly infinite gradations of color during the day, our visual power is limited at night; nevertheless, other beauty reveals itself to us. One of the most magnificent shows are the fireflies of the summer solstice, for then they are in their greatest abundance. Near midnight on June 30, 1996, my unaided eyes perceived an atmosphere full of thousands of fuzzy blinking white lights. I have always been an observer of fireflies, their tiny pinpoints of light rising from the grass at dusk, but I had never seen a light show this spectacular. I stood mesmerized for several minutes before going to put on my glasses. The pointillist blinking lights were even more beautiful than the impressionist ones had been. Throughout the back lawn and beyond, a galaxy of fireflies sent their amorous signals to each other in one of the most beautiful courtship displays on earth. The cottonwood leaves rustled with a sound like falling rain. Horses snuffled near the fence. Tree frogs chirred. Bullfrogs croaked. Surely the true God lives in the natural world, not in some extraterrestrial place.

In later years the vast galaxies of fireflies dwindled. Thinking that pesticides might be to blame, I contacted an entomologist from the Ohio Agricultural Research and Development Center in Wooster who told me that fireflies overwinter in tree bark and underground where pesticides usually do not penetrate. Internet sites, however, suggest that pesticides have taken their toll on the firefly population. Lately I have noticed a resurgence in their numbers, although they have not recovered the multitudes I observed in the late 1990s.

While I have always been a birder, I came to appreciate butterflies more recently, when I left a section of white clover in my riding area unmowed because honeybees were feeding on the flowers. By late summer a mass of butterflies clung to seed heads on long stems. The next spring I planted zinnias, sunflowers, and wildflowers in the garden and the very first year witnessed a profusion of butterflies as well as honeybees and bumblebees. The flowers appear to dance with the movements of colorful wings opening and closing as the butterflies feed on the blossoms. Seeming so delicate, they are actually quite agile and pursue their zig-zagging flight patterns with greater speed and at greater altitudes than their fragile wings would seem to allow.

Spring azure and brown elfins appear earliest in summer. A small yellow butterfly I have never been able to identify inhabits my garden as well as cabbage butterflies, which are probably responsible for tiny pinholes in spinach leaves. The colorful Baltimore—black with white and orange spots—is an early visitor. Wild asters blooming in July attract the Harris's checkerspot, which is orange with many white spots. Among my favorites, the black-and-orange pearl crescents drink at mud puddles throughout the summer. The "eyed" butterflies that hover close to the ground are the little wood satyr, wood nymph, and eyed brown. The multicolored painted lady, question mark, and white and red admirals arrive as soon as the garden flowers bloom. Swallowtails appear in July and stay through September—blue spicebush; eastern tiger, the most magnificent with orange wings streaked with black; eastern black, whose wings are ebony lined with white or orange; the green swallowtail, which is actually blue; and the giant, which is mostly black with distinctive white markings. In October we see the bright-orange Milbert's tortoiseshell, pearly eye, and buckeye with its blue and orange spots and its white-and-red Indian paint. Although numbers of monarchs and viceroys are dwindling, we have both species daily from June until October feeding on zinnias in the garden and ironweed in the pasture. Their orange and black wings remind me of panes of stained glass.

Wasps build their nests along the garage overhang and near fences. I am stung at least once a year, but I don't tear down their houses because they eat tomato worms and other insects that infest the garden. The black and auburn woolly bears appear in late autumn. Insects that infest the garden include corn worms, which I deal with by pulling them off the stalks, and the European corn borer, which I get rid of by cutting off the tips of the corn. Grasshoppers are present from late summer until the first frost. Japanese beetles seem to confine their menus to leaves of flowers past bloom time. I get rid of Mexican bean beetles and yellow, fuzzy saltmarsh caterpillars by brushing them off the bean leaves and dumping them into the field. Since I began rotating broccoli, I have seen few of the tiny green worms that crawl inside the flowerets.

Far from eluding us, the wild batters at our walls and windows. Bees, wasps, and hornets sometimes choose our roof overhang to build their nests. In February 1999 a bat found its way in and flew into the living room where it lay on the carpet clicking and squeaking until we caught it in the animal box and released it in the barn to an uncertain night: bats hibernate in winter, and why this one was active I could not know. We sometimes hear bees or mice between the siding and drywall. One September I heard a katydid shrilling so loudly it was audible in the farthest room, where I sat with opened book. I found the curled green leaf of its body clinging upright to the back window screen where the breeze filtered through. It did not fly when I approached. The natural world was calling to me loudly from some place beyond my understanding.

Sometimes the wild encounters me silently. One night in November I returned from my late class at about 10:30. As I stepped out of my truck, I saw something move above me, a ghostly creature flying among the rafters of the garage. In the dim illumination of the truck's dome light, it fluttered above and around the beams—perhaps a screech owl or barn owl. It fluttered among the shadows, out the door, and into the night with a full moon shining on the barn among dark hills, the point of the roof resembling a ship's prow forging through high waves. I had always wanted to observe an owl close up. As it winged away into the night, I remembered Peter Matthiessen's words in *The Snow Leopard* that the wild creature we seek will reveal itself only when we are ready to see it.

Chapter Seven

John Chapman, 1774–1845

FIVE MILES WEST of my place lies the site where the native village called Greentown stood overlooking the Black Fork River. I knew the location was close but did not know exactly where until the local Johnny Appleseed Memorial Society placed a sign on Route 39 two miles north of Perrysville. One October day in 2006, I parked my truck in front of an old barn and followed a tractor path westward through farmland and woods to the river. My interest lay in the historical significance of the place but also in the character of John Chapman, popularly known as Johnny Appleseed, whom I had read about and knew to be much more interesting than the cartoon character that popular culture has made of him. He had lived for a while in the territory that became Jefferson County, where I grew up, later migrating to Licking County, where I also lived, and then north to what is now Ashland County, my current home. In a way, I followed his footsteps.

The Memorial Society's sign explains that instability among the native people resulted from military expeditions into the area after the Revolutionary War. Some Delaware and Mingo joined many Shawnee who moved as early as 1788 to the place named Greentown for Thomas Green of Connecticut, a Tory who migrated westward and lived among the Shawnee. John Chapman, local preacher James Copus, the Shawnee chief called the Prophet, and a Delaware leader called Captain Pipe frequently visited the settlement, which by 1812 included more than 150 dwellings.

In 2013 the Johnny Appleseed Memorial Society bought the land on which Greentown stood and created a theme park with a log house (built in imitation of Shawnee lodges) and wooded trails leading to sites where the native people cooked and boiled sugar maple syrup. Years earlier, in the Muskingum Watershed Conservancy District of Ashland County, about two miles south of the village of Mifflin, a group called the Johnny Appleseed Heritage Center Inc., headed by a local man named William Smith, had built an outdoor drama park on 118 acres of "managed" forest. Smith also built on the property a naturally contoured amphitheater with a seating capacity of sixteen hundred; an indoor auditorium; an interactive, handicapped-accessible museum; and a learning center. The project received both public and private funds from, among others, the J. M. Smucker Company in nearby Orrville (which makes jams and jellies) and the Ohio Arts and Sports Facilities Commission. The entire complex, opened in 2004, hosted an annual festival and presented living history reenactments similar to those at Schoenbrunn Village near New Philadelphia in Tuscarawas County. Due to financial difficulties, the performances were discontinued after 2006.

Let me state here that this will not be a diatribe against historical theme parks or the effort to create popular history from fragments of a romanticized past. I rejoice at the conservation of 118 wooded acres, which may become old-growth forest. My few objections to outdoor drama and theme parks stem from their oversimplification and often sanguine revisionism, yet ultimately they may inform and spark curiosity.

Given the contemporary appetite for outdoor drama and historical theme parks, I wonder that this one arrives on the scene so recently. Johnny Appleseed embodied one of the enduring myths of the Northwest Territories, and he has been, like Daniel Boone, Davey Crockett, and Kit Carson, transformed by popular culture into a mythic frontiersman who helped bring civilization to the wilderness. Popularization, of course, eliminates the failures, frustrations, and inconsistencies of a life—in short, what makes it interesting. Like the others mentioned, John Chapman led a life far more complex than that created by the entertainment industry.

The man who came to be known as Appleseed John was born in Leominster, Worcester County, Massachusetts, on September 26, 1774, the second child and eldest son of Nathaniel Chapman, a minuteman of Leominster during the Revolutionary War, and Elizabeth Simonds Chapman. After Elizabeth's death in 1776, Nathaniel married Lucy Cooley of Connecticut Valley. They lived at Longmeadow and raised ten more children, five girls and five boys. We know a surprising amount of detail about John Chapman due to biographies such as Robert Price's *Johnny Appleseed: Man and Myth* (1967), Henry A. Pershing's *Johnny Appleseed and His Time: An Historical Romance* (1930), and Newell Dwight Hillis, *The Quest of John Chapman: The Story of a Forgotten Hero* (1904).

Michael Pollan, in *The Botany of Desire* (2001), advances the hypothesis that Chapman primarily contributed not apples but wine to the frontier. Chapman grew trees from seed, not grafting; since apples grown from seed are not good for eating but rather for cidering, and since preservation in those days meant fermentation, Chapman grew apples to be used for wine making. He represents for Pollan a frontier Dionysus. Hugh Nissenson makes Chapman a secondary character in *The Tree of Life* (1983), a frontier novel that examines the intersection of religious faith and savagery and probes the psychology of those professing a religion of love while committing atrocities for the purpose of acquiring land. Nissenson makes Chapman a disaffected son who hates his itinerant father, a thief and proud Revolutionary War veteran who lovingly cleans his gun every Sunday but fails to provide for his children. Grown to manhood, Chapman leaves Massachusetts to escape him. Price, on the other hand, indicates that Chapman kept in touch with his family members, who moved westward to what is now Marietta, Ohio, to join him. Pershing proposes that Chapman spent the years 1787–88 as a missionary with minister Ave Buckles in the Potomac area in Virginia. He also attributes Chapman's emigration westward to a disappointed love affair with a woman named Sarah Crawford who moved with her family to the Ohio country. Hillis identifies the unattainable lady as Dorothy Durand, while Price corroborates neither liaison.

What seems clear is that by the age of twenty-three Chapman had arrived in western Pennsylvania, the scene of land feuds and Indian retaliations, that he had built a cabin near Pittsburgh in 1792, and that by 1797, at twenty-nine, he had sold it and gone to Ohio. "Settlement" in those days involved clearing two acres of every hundred-acre parcel and building a house. Although land was granted to war veterans in lieu of payment for services, such deeds were subject to claim jumping and fraud. Then, as now, laws helped to make big speculators wealthy while giving inadequate protection to small farmers whose land was often taken by concerns such as the Holland Land Company and the Ohio Company. The successful land speculator was often ambitious and ruthless when it came to exploiting people who had little ready cash. When powerful interests of one group, however, take the land and livelihood of the less powerful, the latter often turn not on their oppressors but on some other dispossessed or disadvantaged group. In 1797 the dispossessed white settlers looked toward the land held by native dwellers.

Among those embittered victims of land speculation, John Chapman headed westward, taking with him the craft of nurseryman, which he learned in Pennsylvania. He was not the first: Ebenezer Zane, who was to found Zanesville in 1799, had planted an orchard on Wheeling Island. In search of cheap land, Chapman entered the Ohio country at George's Run, four miles south of what is now Steubenville, and planted orchards there as well as at Zanesville, Newark, the Licking River area, Muskingum watershed, Coshocton, Mount Vernon, Mansfield, and Ashland (then called Uniontown) as he headed north and west.

Chapman was slender, about five feet nine inches tall, with long black hair, a beard, and piercing blue eyes that, legend has it, captivated people. In winter he donned a full-length Quaker coat and felt hat. He wore cast-off clothing, an ankle-length collarless coat of tow linen, straight sleeves inserted into armholes, and usually no shoes. While this type of dress was not uncommon for frontiersmen, by 1818 people had begun to comment on his raggedness and eccentricity. The commonly reproduced figure, and the only one extant, of Chapman as a tall, thin, unkempt man with kind eyes was drawn by a student at Oberlin College who allegedly saw John Chapman in his older days. No other portrait has been found. Chapman's legend includes his respect for all life to the extent that he would not molest a rattlesnake and or chase a sow bear from a hollow log that would have afforded shelter on a winter night. His actions, however, seem less reverent than commonsensical: surely no right-thinking person would molest a rattlesnake, and sow bear are said to be among the most ferociously protective mothers.

The legend further describes an itinerant man moving among his orchards and accepting hospitality from settlers in return for apple seeds and seedlings. He was not itinerant, however: he owned land near George's Run; in Belmont County near the head of Big Stillwater Creek; in Wellsburg, Virginia (now West Virginia); and in Licking County, Ohio, on Scotland Farm, three miles north of Newark. He also owned town lots in Mount Vernon. Toward the end of his life, Price suggests, Chapman may himself have become a land speculator.

Price describes other colorful and eccentric characters of the frontier, such as James Craig, a hard-drinking settler who fought a landowner named Joseph Walker near Mount Vernon. Known today as "Ohio's Colonial Town" because of its well-maintained Victorian houses and picturesque center, and home of the conservative Nazarene College, Mount Vernon was at the end of the eighteenth century an unruly settlement. Newark was even more notorious. Frontier people, young at the time of the Revolution and pinning their hopes on a new Eden in the wilderness, endured severe winters and malarial summers; hardened by frontier life and embittered by losing their land to speculators and their families to retaliations by indigenous people, they skinned wolves alive, cleaned out viper nests and flung the carcasses onto mounds, drank corn whiskey, and amused themselves by witnessing public whippings. John Chapman, who seems to have had some refinement, referred to Newark as "hell."

Six miles westward, the village of Granville had a different evolution. When I lived there from 1986 to 1993, I attended many of the community festivals; every one included amateur historians telling stories, playing mountain dulcimers, and singing about the days of the original settlers who emigrated from Granville, Massachusetts, in a group that included a mayor, town planner, engineer, blacksmith, and minister as well as craftsmen. A temperance community, its people learned the value of minding their own business: when one of them went to Newark to preach against drinking, he was hanged in the street. Even today these two towns retain the flavor of their origins. Granville, a quiet residential village with a strong sense of its own history, boasts stately Victorian houses, old trees, wide central boulevard, public gardens, historic cemetery, strict building codes, regular community festivals at holidays and sugar-maple time, bicycle trail, restrictions on alcohol sales, and the prestigious Denison University located on a hill above the town with a white steeple lit up at night (which students refer to as the "nipple of knowledge"). Newark, on the other hand, now a small industrial city transected by I-70 and affected by urban sprawl and crime, retains its raw image.

Writers on Chapman's life all testify to the grim brutality of the frontier. Using details from Price's biography of Chapman, Nissenson graphically portrays the scalpings, slow torture, and live burnings committed by both settlers and pre-settlement people. He describes a technique documented at the time and repeated in James Fenimore Cooper's *The Last of the Mohicans* of sticking blazing pine needles into human flesh. Reprisals occurred frequently: for example, men named McCullogh and Morrison hunted down native dwellers in revenge for the death of missionary Adam Payne, with no evidence of who his killers were. George Carpenter murdered Indians, even those who had been converted by Moravian missionaries, and met his own death when, during a nightmare, he leaped into a kettle of boiling maple-sugar water.

Native Americans fared worst of all. Decimated by disease brought by seventeenth-century French explorers, their numbers steadily decreased in the Ohio country in the late eighteenth century. Those who remained included Shawnee to the central and northern parts of the territory and Delaware, or Lenni-Lenape ("the original people"), to the east. Gen. George Rogers Clark led an army against the Shawnee and Gen. "Mad" Anthony Wayne against a coalition of nations at the Battle of Fallen Timbers on the Maumee River in 1794. The Treaty of 1795 followed, after which many Native Americans moved north and west. Cornstalk, a Shawnee chief, tried to convince young warriors that they would never defeat the whites. He was nevertheless imprisoned by settlers and assassinated for killing a man named Gilmore, even though he was innocent of the crime. Other Shawnee placed no faith in the treaties of white men. Tecumseh and the Prophet, both Shawnee chiefs, refused to sign and continued to lead war parties against settlers. The Prophet's followers were defeated at Tippecanoe in 1811, and, after allying large numbers of mostly Shawnee and Creek from all over the eastern part of the continent, Tecumseh was killed in the Battle of the Thames in Ontario in 1813.

Not all settlers believed in exterminating or deporting the native dwellers. John Heckewelder, a Moravian missionary in Pennsylvania and later in Ohio, wrote of the generous spirit and quality of life of the Delaware and Shawnee. Chiefs ruled by wise council and reason, he recorded. Parents never scolded or punished children. They possessed no ambition to acquire more than their neighbors or more than they needed. Their varied diet included game, fruit, nuts, vegetables, corn, and fish.

Hostilities raged in 1812, brought on in part by new hope of an alliance between the Shawnee and the British against the Americans. Reverend James Copus, hoping to avert trouble between settlers and indigenous people, urged the inhabitants of Greentown to move to the Mansfield area, having received assurances from white authorities that Shawnee property would be respected. As soon as the Indians departed in August 1812, however, white settlers invaded Greentown, urinated on the floor of the council house, and burned all lodges and possessions. Price includes the detail of the white men using an Indian scalp from which to drink a mixture of blood and whiskey. Reverend Copus, who had been innocent of the whites' intentions, was murdered for misinforming the Shawnee. Settlers made a sweep of the area, killing all Shawnee who remained, although the Copus family's murderers were never precisely identified.

These atrocities provoked Delaware and Shawnee retaliation in a series of raids. The so-called Panic of September 1812 resulted in the settlers of Ashland and Richland Counties abandoning their homes and gathering in the Mansfield blockhouse for safety. John Chapman made journeys over several nights to warn them of expected Shawnee retaliation. As things turned out, most of the evacuations were unnecessary, but on August 10, 1813, a storekeeper named Levi Jones was attacked and killed just north of Mansfield. Once again, fearing continued attacks, settlers gathered into two Mansfield blockhouses. John Chapman volunteered to go to Mount Vernon, about twenty-eight miles away, to notify soldiers and bring reinforcements. No one is sure whether he walked and ran the distance barefoot as legend has it or whether he rode a horse.

Chapman's actions in warning the settlers indicate his loyalty to them, but it is clear that he also lived among the Shawnee who regarded him as a medicine man who could cure blindness. Pershing states that the Shawnee believed him to be possessed by a sacred spirit. Nissenson portrays him as a friend to a young Shawnee warrior who had been unable to communicate with the spirits as was required of him. In the novel, Chapman tells the young warrior to "make God pity [him]" by subjecting himself to inhuman privations. As a result, the Shawnee is visited by the most militant of the spirits and goes on the warpath against all whites except John Chapman. Whatever the literal truth, it is clear that Chapman traveled safely among the Shawnee.

Chapman's spirituality, however, involved more than the Shawnee interpretation of his medicine or the settlers' thinking of him as eccentric. The generation that followed the middle border demonstrated an eagerness for religion in many forms. In the Ohio Valley in the late eighteenth and early nineteenth centuries, many religious groups had already arrived, including Methodists, Moravians, Calvinists, and Unitarians. Settlers near Steubenville are said to have practiced witchcraft. Revivalism, characterized by literalism and emotional demonstrativeness, provided escape from the grimness of pioneer life. John Chapman brought Swedenborgianism, a mystic philosophy neither demonstrative nor simple.

Emanuel Swedenborg (1688–1772), a Swedish geologist, came to believe that God had revealed to him alone the true doctrine of Christianity. He set forth his "Teachings of the New Church" in 1757, when he believed that Christ had come again to earth. Swedenborg describes in his many religious tracts his visitations by angels and his visions of heaven. Although he had not intended to found a new church, his followers initiated the Church of the New Jerusalem after his death.

Swedenborgian mystical philosophy involves the belief in correspondences between this world and the spiritual one. Neoplatonic in its dualism of nature and spirit, Swedenborgianism insists that human beings lived *at once* in the natural and spiritual worlds. The true significance of the scriptures, Swedenborg taught, can be understood by human beings only through the "correspondences" between these two worlds:

> The whole world corresponds to the spiritual world, not only collectively, but in every part; and therefore, whatever exists in the natural world from the spiritual, is said to be the *correspondent* of that from which it exists; . . . Since man is a heaven, and also a world, in least form after the image of the greatest, therefore in him there is a spiritual world and a natural world. The interiors,

which are of his mind, and have reference to understanding and will, constitute his spiritual world; but the exteriors, which are of his body, and have reference to his senses and actions, constitute his natural world.

Swedenborg's doctrine, similar to Platonic philosophy, teaches that what human beings perceive in the visible, or material, world has a correspondence in the invisible, or spiritual, world and postulates the interdependence of heaven and earth. Not only does he avow the necessity of the heavenly to the earthly, as most Christians would; he also and just as firmly avows the necessity of earth for heaven, declaring that the divine is visible in the here and now, in the physical nature of things. While many Christians argue that the material world, whether human-created or natural, can lead human beings away from the spiritual, Swedenborg's insistence on the physical world as essential to the very existence of the spiritual and his descriptions of angels that possess human, not divine, form reveal in certain passages a fascination with the body. He advances the iconoclastic notion that man can be fit for heaven only by means of the world, leading to a belief in the holiness of the physical world unacceptable to many Christians, especially those who insist on the notion of earthly depravity and physical life as a punishment to be endured in hopes of heaven.

John Chapman certainly studied Swedenborg's writings. One Swedenborgian circle in Manchester, England, published an article on January 14, 1817, that described him spreading the word in the wilderness. A letter surviving from William Schlatter of Philadelphia to John Chapman discusses their previous correspondence, commencing in 1815, about their faith. Chapman seems to have lived a double life among humane, literary Swedenborgians and tough, often illiterate frontier people. The notion that people reap what they sow and are known by their fruits may describe Chapman's beliefs. The people of the frontier may have been particularly receptive to the idea that the earth is necessary to the spiritual world since settlers' close relationship to the earth made them conscious of their dependence on it. A nurseryman had to know about seasonal variation, soil quality, and availability of water. It is not clear whether Chapman's husbandry preceded his philosophy or vice versa. Perhaps this grower's faith in nature and the Swedenborgian concept that trees correspond to perception of and knowledge of good and truth led Chapman to embrace the philosophy. Louis Bromfield writes in *Pleasant Valley* that Chapman's Swedenborgian doctrine "changed imperceptibly into a kind of pagan faith which ascribed spirits to trees and sticks and stones and regarded the animals and the birds as his friends." Love of the physical world and belief that everything in it is holy resembles the Shawnee and Delaware belief that the world contained sacred places, that a person could not comprehend sacredness until he or she entered the place, that larks heard human prayer, that thrushes bore the spirits of those long dead, and that certain bodies of water such as lakes and streams contained transforming powers.

Like Chapman and the Swedenborgians, I am convinced that we live at once in the physical and spiritual, and furthermore that the spiritual depends on the physical and cannot exist separately. As I walked between rows of corn and into the woods in the area where Greentown had been, I hoped to feel the presence of ancient inhabitants. The wide grassy path dipped as it entered the trees, beginning to turn gold and red, before climbing a hill into a clearing; the settlement must have extended far down the hillside toward the river in order to have accommodated 150 dwellings. As I stood watching, two white-tailed does stepped from the woods to the north, paused, took the measure of my stillness, and faded into the rows of corn far down the slope. Small white cumulus clouds had begun to build up from the west. I wanted no further visions than the fiery autumn trees above corn waiting to be harvested beneath an ever-changing cloud cover, no further miracles than the seasons.

Chapman can be understood only as a complex personality at once bitter and hopeful, cynical and altruistic, frustrated and determined. He possessed strong desire and energy as well as wanderlust. Unable to settle down anywhere, he kept moving northwest, dying near Fort Wayne, Indiana, in 1845 at the age of seventy-one. Having no permanent home, he was better able to be at home everywhere. The facts of this fascinating, enigmatic man's life challenge the simplistic icon still being represented of John Chapman as a comical, kindly missionary—a cliché supported more by propaganda than historical evidence. The woods around the Greentown memorial and the heritage center may mature into old-growth forest, which will stand more fittingly than any outdoor drama or theme park for the heritage of John Chapman.

Chapter Eight

Bridge of Dreams

HONEY CREEK BEGINS about five miles north of our place and runs due south until it meets the Black Fork of the Mohican River. The watershed of about one hundred square miles includes four tributaries—Clear Fork, Black Fork, Jerome Fork, and Muddy Fork—flowing from the north to join the Lake Fork, which becomes the major part of the river. The Mohican in turn joins the Kokosing River to become the Walhonding, itself a major tributary of the Muskingum, which runs south from Coshocton to Zanesville, then southeast toward Marietta where it empties into the Ohio River. The Ohio flows southwestward until it joins the Mississippi at the southern tip of Illinois.

The village of Loudonville calls itself the "Canoeing Capital of Ohio" because of its location on the Mohican. According to local journalist and naturalist Irv Oslin, a man named Dick Frye established a canoe livery in 1961 and transformed Loudonville into a resort area. In the 1970s and '80s, however, there were few people paddling the river or camping in the park. Today the stretch of the Clear Fork that flows parallel to Ohio State Route 3 southeast of the village is crowded with motels, camping facilities, canoe liveries, carnival rides, water slides, and restaurants. Still, at Frye's Landing the river becomes less civilized. Greenville, once a commercial center and stop on the Walhond-

The Bridge of Dreams, Knox County, Ohio (Photo © Chad Wilkins)

ing Valley Railroad, now boasts only a few houses and a church. Downstream, the river meanders past steep, forested hills and farms. After Brinkhaven Road Bridge, at a bend called Alum Rock, the canoeist sees stunning rocky outcroppings some three hundred feet high.

The most natural section of the Mohican, eighteen miles of the Lake Fork from Brinkhaven to the Mohawk Dam, traverses a gradually widening valley densely forested and inhabited by much wildlife. Canoeists and hikers can sight bald eagles, belted kingfishers, cedar waxwings, great blue herons, green herons, and wood ducks. Alert observers spot beaver, muskrats, river otters, and white-tailed deer. Ospreys perch in high branches waiting for the fish that swim to the surface in the wake of passing canoes. Brinkhaven was a thriving community until disasters of biblical proportion caused its people to leave: the great flood of 1913 washed away its woolen mill, and a fire in 1951 destroyed the gristmill. Another settlement on this fork,

Frye's Landing, on the Mohican River (Photo © Irv Oslin)

Cavallo, once a commercial stop on the canal route, became a ghost town when the railroad rendered the canals obsolete by 1896. Brinkhaven Dam produces a churning turbulence, and drownings were not infrequent (as many as eight people in a single summer) until a section was carved out with jackhammers to make the passage safer.

Near Brinkhaven, in Knox County, a covered bridge said to be the second longest in the state (370 feet) and the third longest in the country spans the Mohican River. Covered bridges are nothing new in Ohio, which contains 142 of them, the second largest number in the country after Pennsylvania's 219. Many of Ohio's covered bridges are modern, but most were first constructed in the nineteenth century and have since been remodeled, updated, or repaired. A former railroad trestle constructed in the 1920s, the bridge near Brinkhaven joins sections of the Mohican Valley Trail, built on the abandoned right-of-way belonging to the old Pennsylvania Railroad. Closed to motorized traffic, it is used by hikers, cyclists, and Amish buggies. When local people developed a plan to cover the bridge, skeptics claimed they were "dreaming." The planners proved that they could make their dream come true by raising the ninety thousand dollars needed for the project. When the bridge was dedicated in 1999, they named it the "Bridge of Dreams."

The Clear Fork of the Mohican River runs thirty-six miles past varied landscapes, including a former gold prospecting camp. The bottom is rock, gravel, and sand with natural riffles and pools, which make it one of the highest-quality fishing streams in the state. On its banks, Newville became a ghost town when the B&O Railroad carried its business away by building tracks through Butler and Perrysville. Another abandoned community, Helltown—named for the German word for "clear" and home to both pioneers and Native Americans—was abandoned in 1782 when the Delaware moved to Greentown after learning of the massacre at Gnadenhutten of native people converted to the Moravian faith. One favorite part of this tributary is the nearly five-mile stretch called Clear Fork Gorge where hills covered with mature conifers and hardwoods rise three hundred feet from a valley one thousand feet wide. Placed on the National Registry of Natural Landmarks by the National Park Service, the gorge can be viewed from below in a canoe or above from a ridge where the forested slope plummets steeply to the stream; on the other side, a succession of hills rises green and blue into the distance. This part of the forest is off-limits to hiking, so there are no footpaths descending the steep hillside.

If quiet is the place where one can listen fifteen minutes and not hear a human-created sound, then there are quiet places on the Mohican River and in the surrounding forest. One trail offering varied terrain and forest ecosystems follows the north side of the river from the state park headquarters and passes near the Clear Fork Gorge State Nature Preserve before terminating at Pleasant Hill Dam. One of the more challenging hiking trails—and consequently less traveled—begins at the fire tower and traverses four miles through part of the state forest to the modern covered bridge at State Route 97. From there to Charles

Mill Lake, the trail follows the river through the Mohican State Park and reveals spectacular vistas, large trees, rocky outcroppings, and two waterfalls (Big and Little Lyons Falls) but also many more hikers and picnickers, as this is most visitors' favorite part. While the park boasts only about eight miles of well-used trails, the forest contains about fifty miles of less-visited paths dedicated to snowmobiling and horseback riding but which hikers can also use to take them into back country with varied forest ecologies, cliffs and gorges only slightly less spectacular than those in the park, and openings that reveal rolling countryside and farmland. Along parts of the trail, one can imagine the awe as well as fear that pioneers must have felt when riding or walking through those deep woods. One of the longer bridle trails passes an old church now boarded up and standing near the tiny Sand Ridge Cemetery, established in 1803 and containing many weathered headstones with indecipherable names and dates. Veteran back country hikers who know the forest well have identified evidence of native and pioneer dwellings. Local naturalists call it "a little piece of Canada" because glaciers, pushing the soil southward, stopped at the Mohican hills, where observers now can spot cerulean warblers and other songbirds usually seen farther north.

On the Black Fork of the Mohican, Charles Mill Lake—1,350 acres in size, with thirty-four miles of shoreline—appears natural but is not. Constructed in 1938, the Charles Mill Dam, one of fourteen built along the Muskingum Watershed by the US Army Corps of Engineers, turned three rather deep natural lakes (about fifty to one hundred feet) into one large body of water only about eight feet in depth. Nevertheless, with its resident populations of eagles, ospreys, egrets, and herons and visited by migrating sandhill cranes and white pelicans, the lake looks beautiful in any season.

Natural history is omnipresent in this area, although few people know it. The greatest "natural" disaster in Ohio history was the flood of 1913, caused by four days of torrential rain over land that had been robbed of its forest cover throughout the nineteenth century, which left about 450 people dead and two hundred fifty thousand homeless. Downtown Dayton, the hardest hit municipality, lay covered by twenty feet of water. In response, the Ohio General Assembly created four flood-control districts, of which the Muskingum Watershed Conservancy District, organized in 1933, served eastern Ohio—about 20 percent of the state's total area, or nearly eight thousand square miles. The districts are governed by boards of directors chosen by judges in the counties included in the region, but day-to-day operations are carried out by seven board-appointed "executives" who are mostly not known by the people living in the district. As of this writing, the chief of conservation, whose term began in 2018, is a person who worked in the oil and gas industry for sixteen years.

The entire Mohican Complex includes nine thousand acres of forest and parkland consisting of the Mohican State Park and Forest, Pleasant Hill Lake State Park, and Malabar Farm State Park, with spectacular geological formations, mature forests, prairie tracts, and waterfalls such as Hemlock and Big Lyons Falls. Conservation easements preserved 579 acres in Richland County alone. A new trail, opened in 2015, links the Richland B&O Trail and others to the Mohican, fortunately off-limits to all-terrain vehicles and dirt bikes.

The Mohican State Forest, located in Richland and Ashland Counties, consists of 4,525 acres of abused and abandoned farmland reseeded and replanted by the Civilian Conservation Corps. The restored forest contains some of the most valuable timber in the state, a fact not lost on wood and paper companies who try to convince sympathetic legislators to allow them to log in public land under the rubric of "management" and even in the Shrine Memorial Forest Park set aside to honor fallen veterans. Timber company representatives even describe clear-cutting disingenuously as "imitation of a natural process," since lightning sometimes clears out sections of forests, but their reasoning overlooks the fact that natural processes are not planned. Over the last twenty-five years, I have participated in a number of demonstrations at the forest shrine or the Sand Ridge Cemetery to save parts of the Mohican from logging, mostly friendly gatherings where Forest Service officials and State Highway Patrolmen mingled with demonstrators. Now this land is under threat not only from logging and mining but more recently from oil and gas exploration and horizontal hydraulic fracturing.

The Department of Forestry (DOF) unveiled a new plan in 2017 to log forty acres of mature woods because, it claims, the white and red pines planted in the 1940s are not indigenous to the area; although the land had been twice thinned of pines, they claim that new logging would allow the more valuable hardwoods to grow back. Yet areas that were clear-cut in 2008 with the purpose of restoring indigenous ecology have not grown back in hardwoods but in sassafras and bush honeysuckle, invasive species that even the DOF, currently headed by a former timber company "resource forester," admits it does not have staff enough to remove. The state allows periods of public commentary, and DOF officials hold public hearings, but often in rooms too small to accommodate all the people who attend and sometimes employing strategies such as not allowing public questioning—they claim, because such opportunities can become "confrontational."

We need a new dream for this watershed and its entire ecosystem—a dream that includes preservation of old growth forests, diversified ecosystems, and love of the land even if it still bears its human-created scars.

Chapter Nine

Thrill of the Chase

IT'S 8:00 A.M. on a Saturday in early September in Carroll County, Ohio. Birdsong rings out from tall poplars reflected in a still pond beside the trail. The headmaster sounds the horn, and brown, black, and white foxhounds spill out in a stream from a kennel truck and set off before us at a trot with their tails high. Riders follow—master of foxhounds, whippers-in, and field masters, followed by senior members and jumpers. Newer members and non-jumpers ride at the rear. The masters wear the bright scarlet coats, called "pink" by those in the sport, while the others wear black coats; all wear buff or white breeches, black boots, and white cravats.

I have been up for three hours getting my hunter Montana ready and trailering him over to the fixture, the farm where the hunt members gather. The morning is cool—about fifty degrees—and dry, so both horses and riders feel excited and eager to go. Sugar maple leaves blaze scarlet, and white oaks are beginning to turn yellow. The deciduous trees contrast with the dark green of hemlock and white pine, the slate blue of spruce, the bright green of hayfields, rusty brown of soybeans, and the gold of the oat straw left after harvesting. The horn sounds again followed by melodious clopping of hooves on gravel.

Those in the lead begin to trot, and we start down a grassy lane between a briar-encircled stone fence and a wooden one with trees alongside it. Horses left in the pasture whinny to our mounts and gallop up to the fence, but we leave them behind as we canter to a coop, a triangle-shaped wooden box about three feet at the apex. Riders space themselves three or four lengths behind the one in front and take the jump in their turn. Others go around. Montana loves jumping and takes this one eagerly. Horses usually enjoy a hunt because they feel safest in large groups, and all their instincts tell them to run with a herd.

Fog rises from a rocky gray stream. We stop to cross the water singly, and I hear the sound of iron horseshoes on stone. The sun has come from behind the enormous cumulus clouds, and it looks like fair weather all morning—which means a better ride but worse hunting because hounds can pick up the scent of a fox more easily during slight rain. We trot in single file along a dry path through woods, jumping over small downed tree trunks.

The cry "Low bridge!" means a low-hanging tree branch ahead.

We stop and regroup, then pick up the pace again and soon are out of the woods and cantering along the side of a cornfield, then over a small coop into a meadow.

"Ware holes," someone yells, a contraction of "Beware of the holes," which could be groundhog dens but more likely soft depressions in the turf. We gallop about a half mile around the edge of green fields, the hillside rising on one side and woods on the other. For the first time those of us in the middle can see all the horses in front—bays, chestnuts, and grays following hounds that have found a scent.

Hounds enter the woods again but lose the trail. Foxes are intelligent animals and know where they are pursued and where they are safe; hunters sometimes see them sitting complacently on top of wood piles or tool sheds in backyards where they know we are not allowed to follow.

Foxhunting as we know it began in England in the seventeenth century using hounds developed from French breeds that weighed sixty to seventy pounds and stood about two feet at the shoulder. The slightly smaller American foxhound was bred in the eighteenth century by Virginia settlers, the sport having come to America with English colonists. Almost all eastern states have foxhunting clubs; the oldest in the country is located in Geneseo, New York, while Virginia boasts the Museum of Hounds and Hunting in Leesburg as well as the largest number of organized clubs, including the prestigious Middleburg and Orange County Hunts, where Jacqueline Kennedy rode. The sport remains very small, with only about ten thousand people nationwide hunting regularly. For a short time in the early nineteenth century, foxhunting became so fast and dangerous that women were excluded, but this changed when the bold riding of Elizabeth of Austria dispelled prejudice against women equestrians. By 1930 women hunted in equal numbers with men, usually riding astride rather than sidesaddle.

The favorite horse for hunting is the Thoroughbred, although many riders prefer to cross the racing-type horse with stockier breeds like the Quarter Horse or Connemara. Some even cross the Thoroughbred with draft breeds like Percherons or Clydesdales. People with more money own German warmblood varieties such as Hanoverians or Trakehners, which are both large and very athletic. Some ride Paints and Appaloosas. Any sound horse that will behave in a large group and wants to jump can be a foxhunter. In Colorado, California, and Washington, people on horseback hunt rabbits with beagles, or they hunt coyotes, and many prefer to ride Arabian horses, which can withstand long gallops in warmer temperatures.

Organized hunts usually have several locations called "fixtures" where the hunts begin, usually farms owned by club members, with permission obtained from surrounding landowners to ride over their property, since public rights-of-way do not exist in the United States as they do in Britain. One thousand to three thousand acres are required to have a fixture. In eastern Ohio, some of the land is absentee-owned, often by factories or mining companies that have ceased operations. Hunt club members put up and maintain the jumps and keep the wooded trails clear.

Strong opposition to hunting in England on humanitarian grounds took the form of disturbing the scent, sabotaging the jumps, and spooking horses. The efforts of the Blair government to end foxhunting brought out people of all classes both in favor of and against hunting. On September 11, 2002, over four hundred thousand people marched peacefully in London not only for hunting but also against what they saw as a threat to their way of life, calling the event "Liberty and Livelihood" and themselves the Countryside Alliance as opposed to the Urban Alliance that worked to eliminate hunting. Foxhunters continued to test and even defy the law that banned all hunting with dogs. Some used eagles instead of hounds, and some hunt as they always had, knowing that police are not inclined to follow groups of riders far into the countryside.

Animosity toward hunting, however, stems as much from class differences as from objection to cruelty: "It's the whole class thing," an Englishwoman explained to me several years ago. "I oppose all class distinctions." The much less vocal opposition in the United States comes from those in groups like People for the Ethical Treatment of Animals (PETA) who not only oppose hunting but also raising animals for food, using them for work, and even keeping them as pets; PETA's philosophy has nothing to do with class differences. Most Americans are unaware of foxhunting except where people live in proximity to a fixture. Class distinctions are no more evident than in any other sport—such as skiing, tennis, golf, or mountain climbing—in which participants must have sufficient income. I have ridden with five organized hunts, and I never experienced class-consciousness; on the contrary, most clubs are eager for new members. Some devoted foxhunters finance their hobby by driving rust-bucket cars and living in modest houses so they can afford to board a horse. It's true that most hunts require several wealthy members in order to provide land to ride over and the wherewithal to support the pack, but I have always found these people gracious and happy to share what they have. I am sure there is class-consciousness in the more prestigious Virginia hunts, but I am guessing no more so than in the other sports I mentioned. Like polo, foxhunting in the United States is for anyone who can ride and afford to own or rent a horse. Far more snobbish in my opinion are people I have been acquainted with who compete in the horse show circuit for points; compared to them, people who ride to hounds are tolerant, accepting, and noncompetitive. Still, foxhunters emulate, if not practice, a way of life of privilege and elegance built on the labor of servants and tenant farmers, so at least the image suggests class-consciousness.

One argument against hunting predators is that they have no power of reason and no choice but to kill their prey; people, supposedly possessing the ability to reason, should not treat animals like adversaries. Predators, moreover, are necessary to trim the populations of prey animals to a size the land will sustain. In one of his most famous essays, "Thinking Like a Mountain," Aldo Leopold warns that killing off predators—in his example, wolves—means disaster for the land as deer browse all edible vegetation until the land becomes a dustbowl. Similarly, foxes help to control the populations of rabbits and small rodents, but their impact on the land is not as dramatic as that of larger predators like mountain lions and wolves, which have helped to restore habitats for many species by controlling deer populations in national parks, most notably Yellowstone.

The irony of foxhunting, however, lies in the fact that it is a dangerous sport, often in cold or wet weather, pursuing something the hunter doesn't really want to catch. Hounds have to be trained to bring the fox to bay in order to have a kill. In northern foxhunts—unlike some in the southern United States, Ireland, and Britain before the 2005 ban—hounds are not usually trained that way but rather pursue the fox in a line until it goes to ground (enters its den), where only a smaller dog like a Jack

Russell terrier can bring it out. Once the fox has gone to ground, the hunt is over. Hunters are now protective not only of the prey but of their habitat, because without foxes there would be no chase and consequently no good riding. During hunts, I have seen several foxes but have never seen a kill—nor would I ride with a hunt in which foxes were killed.

In Great Britain, which has a large population of foxes, shooting them is legal if they become predators. Foxhunters, perhaps spuriously, justify what they do by claiming that being killed by a hound is less cruel than dying a slow, agonizing death in a leghold trap or from wounds inflicted by farmers, who are not always expert marksmen.

An argument against hunting for prey animals—such as deer, rabbits, grouse, or pheasants—is that people now have other ways of getting food and should abandon the barbarism of the hunt on humanitarian grounds. The argument in favor of hunting for prey is that the sport is less cruel than industrial feedlots. Calves pressing their noses to the air holes in the sides of livestock trucks cannot be happier than deer trying to escape from hunters. I suspect that killing one animal at a time for food damages the soul of the hunter far less than mass killing damages the spirit of the worker in the slaughterhouse. Were people closer to their food sources, they might have more respect than they now do for the environment, for those who grow and produce food, and for the entire process of survival, from which too many think they are far removed.

Hunters of many kinds of animals contribute to the environmental movement. Trappers spearheaded the effort to preserve beaver habitat near Lake Erie. Anglers support the Clean Water Act and other legislation that protects game fish. Deer hunters work to save forest, prairie, and wetland habitat. I have heard them voice their opposition to careless development as strongly as birders, hikers, and equestrians. Ted Williams, in his essay "Natural Allies," lists several success stories that resulted from joint efforts of environmentalists and those who hunt and fish. Working on farmland preservation, I found myself the ally of the president of the local rifle association: while we disagree on gun-control legislation, we agree that ecosystems must be preserved and that wilderness has a right to exist for its own sake. The American authority on foxhunting, Alexander MacKay-Smith, writes that the sport "reawakens in us the primitive passion for the chase of wild game with running hounds, a passion which is as old as the human race." He continues:

> Foxhunting offers a liberal education in the mysteries of the scent as affected by temperature, clouds, sunlight, rain and snow; the direction and intensity of the wind; the character and surface of the terrain—woods, streams, grassland and underbrush; the haunts of the foxes and their lines of travel; the telltale warners of their presence—diving crows, fleeing sheep, pursuing cattle; the strategy and boldness of the fox—the line he runs and every irregular twist that will make pursuit difficult for the hounds.

Aldo Leopold himself was an avid bird and deer hunter who came from a family of hunters. Leopold's field was forestry, but his work in New Mexico led him to the study of wildlife, and he wrote the original textbook on game management. In "Wildlife in American Culture" he calls foxhunting "one of the purest of sports; it has real split-rail flavor; it has man-earth drama of the first water."

Henry David Thoreau, who became a vegetarian during his experience in the woods, writes in *Walden* that, because hunting is often a young boy's introduction to the wilderness and often teaches him to love the woods, boys should be taught to hunt, but they should give up the activity when they are older. Not all who hunt as boys are willing to follow Thoreau's advice, of course. Rick Bass maintains in "Why I Hunt" that people in hunter-gatherer cultures probably have richer imaginations than those in agricultural or post-agricultural societies because a hunter's imagination must become engaged with the pursuit—the prey, not the predator, being in control:

The hunted shapes the hunter; the pursuit and evasion of predator and prey are but shadows of the same desire. The thrush
wants to remain a thrush. The goshawk wants to consume the
thrush and in doing so, partly become the thrush—to take its
flesh into its flesh. They weave through the tangled branches of
the forest, zigging and zagging, the goshawk right on the thrush's
tail, like a shadow. Or perhaps it is the thrush that is the shadow
thrown by the light of the goshawk's fiery desire.

Bass romanticizes the experience for thrush and goshawk, but
it is certain that hunting can bring people closer to their natural
condition of subsistence living and thereby bring them more
into sympathy with the wild. He goes on to say that crops will
not seek to elude the farmer, while a deer hunter enters the
woods with nothing but imagination. Farmers must deal with
weather and soil fertility, however, and so I maintain with Louis
Bromfield and Wendell Berry that farmers must be imaginative
and intelligent, no less than hunters. Keeping a garden for just
one year may instill values of thrift and respect for farm work.
Similarly, killing, cleaning, and preparing meat even once could
teach consumers what is involved in the process of survival.

Sport is not the same as subsistence, however; a hunter today knows that the family will not starve if he or she returns
without a deer or bison, and foxhunters do not even wish to
catch what they pursue. The assertion that killing for sport
represents base instincts carries some weight, especially when
hunters use increasingly sophisticated weapons against prey
that cannot develop new means of escape.

Still, foxhunters love the wild and will work to preserve the
way of life that keeps farms from being broken up into subdivi-
sions and forests from being logged. We leave woodpiles on our
land for foxes and build brush coveys for pheasant and quail.
We appreciate the sound of horseshoes on gravel or stone more
than the drone of the internal combustion engine. Foxhunting
is a fast-paced ride over fences through varied country, with
new vistas constantly opening up. It is not competitive, as horse

shows are, yet it is sport, a partnership with one's horse and camaraderie with other riders. Natural-looking coops or logs invite a rider into the mystery of a forest path, field, or dell; stone walls wound with briars reveal the history of a place. Riding, like walking, takes us back to tradition and nature. Few sights are more beautiful than a grassy path weaving among autumn trees or an old rail fence marking the entrance to the woods. They are invitations to enter the spirit of the natural place inhabited for a long time by those who were close to the land.

The hunt is over and we are walking back along those lanes from which we first set forth. The bull thistle's purple crown is in full bloom. At our approach, a great blue heron takes off from the pond and flies high over the trees. Mallards and Canada geese continue to glide along the water. Hounds fan out and trot back to their kennel. The horses walk toward the stable on long reins with lowered heads and swinging gait.

Chapter Ten

Louis Bromfield, Malabar Farm, and Faith in the Earth

ONE OF THE MOST interesting parks in northeastern Ohio is Malabar Farm, founded by Louis Bromfield, the author and farmer who conducted the first American experiment in sustainable agriculture. The estate, now a state park near the little town of Lucas, occupies 580 acres in a valley about twelve miles west of my place. Although the Mohican State Park and Forest provide many more miles of trail riding, the environment there is all deep woods, while the twelve-mile Malabar Farm trail contains both field and forest surroundings and many more changing vistas. From the horse-trailer park, I can survey the hills to the north rising from Pleasant Valley and the deep woods to the south. I particularly like to ride here in the autumn when the leaves of the sugar maples are red, the oaks golden, and the sweet gum fuchsia and copper. September and October are still warm, but flies no longer plague the horses as they do in summer.

I first read Bromfield in high school and heard much about the celebrated farmer-novelist whose name nevertheless has been forgotten by most non-Ohioans. During a camping trip at the Mohican State Park in the 1970s, I found the house by accident as I was driving in the area; having seen its picture in books, I knew at once that I was at Malabar. Sixteen years later I moved here and began to explore the farm in detail.

The bridle trail begins at the edge of a meadow and winds through young deciduous trees, wildflowers, and woody vines down a steep ravine where it enters the woods and continues to a creek. In places the trail is wide and dry, while in some of the lowland places the trail is muddy and obscured by fallen leaves. We canter up an incline, across a meadow of deep purple ironweed and goldenrod, and through the old apple orchard that Bromfield first envisioned providing the farm's cash crop before he abandoned that plan for beef and dairy. At the end of the orchard, the trail leads abruptly down and around a bend into the deeper woods. Here the trail widens and passes through a section of old growth forest with towering sandstone features called "rock cities" rather than "caves." The farm managers have installed plastic tubing to bring the sap from the maple tree stand to the valley where in the winter it is processed into some of the best syrup in the area. I regret that the sap is not gathered in the old way, with buckets on wagons drawn by horses, but state funding does not allow for hiring many workers. The trail winds down a very steep path to the riparian plateau of Switzer Creek, crosses the stream, and climbs the bank to the other side where we ascend a hillside and emerge at the gravel road that leads from the working farm to the Malabar Inn.

The high point of the ride, this part of the bridle trail contains cultural and personal significance. The wide swaths of corn, wheat, alfalfa, and clover remind visitors that Bromfield was one of the first agriculturalists to promote contour farming and return to natural fertilizers. My horse and I pass the pond featured in the chapter of *Malabar Farm* titled "The Life Cycle of a Farm Pond" where I can hear frogs and birds singing and view herons still as reeds, watching for fish. The sky is dazzling cobalt, and cirrus curl upward like the foam on cresting waves. Above the pond stands a small barn where I used to buy hay when I first moved here. Farther to the east are the pastures separated into four "cells" that allow cattle to be rotated; while one area is grazed, the others are allowed to lie fallow so that grass can grow back, and hence the pasture is not overgrazed. Across ant Valley Road, the two-story brick house, built in 1820 to be a stagecoach inn, now serves as a restaurant. Beneath the inn is a farm market where vegetables and fruit grown at Malabar are for sale, kept cool by water that flows from the hillside. Farther down and closer to the barn, a pump invented by Bromfield brings the water back out of the ground, propelled by water pressure, not electricity, in the shadow of an old shed where in Bromfield's day vegetables were sorted and washed for canning.

A side trail crosses Pleasant Valley Road to Mount Jeez where Bromfield gave Sunday lectures on sustainable farming and gardening to hundreds of visitors during the 1940s and 1950s. From the top, the viewer can gaze southward at a 290-degree panorama that includes the rural landscape where five counties meet—Richland, Ashland, Holmes, Knox, and Morrow. The main trail runs along a tractor path between contour-planted rows of corn and alfalfa the length of the working farm, about a half mile, the most exhilarating part of the ride. Here my normally placid trail horse, Dakota, gallops so eagerly that I imagine he dreams he is the reincarnation of Secretariat.

Toward the end of the field, the tractor path turns south toward the barns of the working farm. Across Pleasant Valley Road on private property, a nineteenth century brick schoolhouse is now a dwelling, and for a long time a tree stood in the field, the iconic oak in *The Shawshank Redemption*, under which the character called Red discovers the box Andy has hidden for him. (The tree is now gone, having been stuck by lightning several years ago.) As I head toward the working farm, I pass sheds for tractors, plows, disks, hoes, hay wagons, and other farm implements. The largest barn houses cattle and, formerly, Belgian draft horses that pulled the wagonloads of visitors around the farm. Now tractors pull the wagons. There is also a petting corral where children can become acquainted with sheep, goats, and donkeys; a farm pond below the barns is usually occupied by ducks, mallards, and Canada geese. The working farm office is located here across the road from the white house, now a youth hostel, where the Bromfields lived while their big house was being constructed. We walk past the buildings and the place where volunteers used to keep the Victory Garden planted by Bromfield in memory of one of the customs that helped the Allies prevail in World War II. Farther on we come to the white picket fence surrounding Oliveti Cemetery, a pioneer graveyard dating back to 1820, where Bromfield and his wife, Mary, are buried along with other family members. Once past the cemetery, we swing into a brisk trot past cornfields and pastureland and continue down the gravel road to the point where we entered the working farm.

About a quarter mile away, the great house, featured on calendars and postcards, sits grandly on a hillside across the road from the main barn, which houses exhibits on sustainable farming practices. It is a replica of the one built by Bromfield, rebuilt by the Timber Framers Guild, as the original burned to the ground in 1993 because of faulty wiring in an incubator. Beside the barn, visitors explore a dairy, coops and pens for hens and ducks, interpretive center, and aviary. Behind the house the terraced flower gardens descend to another farm pond. Part of the bridle trail winds behind the house, up a hill, and into the woods. The rider emerges at the top of the hill into a series of alfalfa fields in a large clearing where we can gallop along a tractor path. At the end of the field the trail enters the woods again, emerges onto another part of the expansive alfalfa field, crosses Hastings Road, and then reenters the woods before leading back to the Horsemen's Camp and finally the trailer park.

When asked to contribute to the Dictionary of Literary Biography: Twentieth-Century American Nature Prose Writers (2003), I suggested that my subject be Louis Bromfield whose work I was rereading at the time. The editors had not planned an entry for him, however, and I ended up writing about Aldo Leopold. Bromfield was also excluded from American Nature Writers, an unfortunate omission since Malabar Farm contains eloquent and prescient environmentalist writing, and his six other volumes of non-fiction written between 1945 and 1955—all of which emphasize the necessity of harmony between human beings and the natural order—constitute a significant contribution to the literature of nature. Using the term "ecology" in its current sense long before most writers did, Bromfield devoted his life to restoring the land and healing the rift between industrial society and nature. As a result of his boyhood experience on his grandfather's farm and his own experiment in sustainable agriculture, he produced at least two books that should be included in the canon of environmentalist writing and place him among the ranks of notable literary environmentalists—*Pleasant Valley* (1945) and *Malabar Farm* (1948).

As I read more extensively in the work of Leopold, I was increasingly struck by the similarities between our most famous twentieth century literary ecologist and Bromfield. The narrative structures of both *Malabar Farm* and *Pleasant Valley* recall yearly patterns and focus on the observations of everyday life on the farm as Leopold so eloquently does in *A Sand County Almanac*. Leopold, like Bromfield, also wrote many articles on practical themes, such as attracting songbirds, maintaining fish populations, conserving soil, and protecting old-growth forest. Bromfield, like Leopold, lectured widely on the subjects of conservation and wildlife preservation, and his writings also addressed cultural and moral concerns, although Bromfield traveled around the world while Leopold stayed mostly in the United States, making only one trip abroad to Germany.

Initiating the tradition followed by Wes Jackson and Wendell Berry, Bromfield focused his attention on sustainable farming practices and believed that the farm should resemble as much as possible a natural ecosystem. He also revered the task of farming and thought farmers were among the most intelligent and valuable workers in society. Living within a place and adapting one's life to the ecosystem in which one lives—what poet Gary Snyder calls "being inhabitory"—was as essential to Bromfield as it is to Snyder and Berry; as Berry was to do, Bromfield returned in his later years to farm in the area where he had been born and raised. Like the poet Robinson Jeffers, Bromfield questioned the economic direction that he thought America was taking and believed that true independence meant living within one's ecological means. He also imagined a green economy before environmentalists developed that term. Most of all, Bromfield resembled the quintessential American farmer-author-inventor-philosopher Thomas Jefferson, who envisioned not wealthy men but yeoman farmers as the backbone of the social order and the agrarian life as preferable to any other. Praising Jefferson in *Pleasant Valley* as "our most civilized American," Bromfield alludes to him more than to any other writer and followed his example as an experimental agriculturalist, inventor, political and cultural thinker, Francophile, and believer in an economy based on family farming. He would not have agreed with Jefferson's holding slaves or his refusal to recognize his children by a slave mistress, writing in *Malabar Farm* that the solution to "racial differences and ills" is equal economic opportunity, education, nutrition, better social ethics, and an end to ideas about the superiority of one race over another.

Louis Bromfield, who led one of the most fulfilled and active lives I have ever read about, was a native of Mansfield, Ohio, born in 1896 to Charles Brumfield and Annette Coulter Brumfield, whose ancestors dated back to the original pioneers in Richland County in the north-central part of the state. He claimed that an editor's mistake on a publication changed his name to Bromfield, although some critics have suggested that the idea was his own. Louis gained his love of the land and agriculture from both his father and his grandfather Coulter; from his mother he acquired love of literature and desire to distinguish himself, and in a large extended family he found the prototypes of many fictional characters. His interest in writing was nurtured early when he worked for the city newspaper, where he met people from many backgrounds different from his own. After a year studying agriculture at Cornell, he returned to help on his father's farm. He then chose to study journalism at Columbia, but when the war came he enlisted in the US Army Ambulance Service, seeing much action at close range from 1916 until 1918 and being awarded the Croix de Guerre by the French government. In 1919 he returned to New York and worked for the City News Service, the Associated Press, G. P. Putnam, *Time*, and *The Bookman*. In 1923 he married Mary Appleton Wood, a New England debutante from a family of publishers. His first novel, *The Green Bay Tree* (1924), was an immediate popular success.

Many critics placed Bromfield in the style and tradition of the Victorian novelists and of Balzac, Galsworthy, and Sherwood Anderson. His visit to India in 1932 produced *The Rains Came*, praised by Braj Kishan Koul Agyani, the book's translator into Hindi, as the only novel about India written by an American who demonstrated the sympathy an Indian would have for his own country. Not all critics lavished such compliments, however. Edmund Wilson at *The New Yorker* criticized Bromfield's work severely and claimed that he had not lived up to his early promise. Joseph Wood Krutch wrote that, while Bromfield had the storyteller's art, he did not contribute anything new in situation, character, idea, or point of view. Krutch described Bromfield as having merely a "simple sincere style and a competent narrative method." Marxist critics at *The New Republic* charged that Bromfield was a reactionary Hollywoodite due to the fact that many of his books were made into films (Bromfield himself wrote screenplays and knew many actors, including James Cagney, Lauren Bacall, and Humphrey Bogart), and they misread his novel *A Modern Hero* as praise rather than condemnation of materialism.

Recent critics have reassessed Bromfield's contribution to fiction, stating that his strongest work—most of which was written while he lived in France—conveys the message that human beings must learn to live within the laws of nature and that industrialism destroyed communities and meaningful ways of life.

Like Sherwood Anderson, Bromfield knew how stifling life in small industrial towns could be. His first four novels—*The Green Bay Tree, Possession, Early Autumn* (for which he won the Pulitzer Prize), and *A Good Woman*, which Bromfield suggested could be collected as a "panel" series—all concern the escape from the narrowness of small-town existence but also the increasing alienation of industrialized society from the natural world. The first paragraphs of *The Green Bay Tree* describe a garden walled to keep artificial beauty in and industrial ugliness out. Also like Sherwood Anderson, Bromfield did not believe that escape necessarily meant fulfillment; it often led to alienation. No pastoral idealist, Bromfield believed in embracing the present with all its imperfections.

The *Farm*, Bromfield's semiautobiographical novel, most fully conveys his conviction that the degradation of the earth by industrialism and greed leads to diminishment of society and individual freedom. Some critics have suggested that this novel embodies Bromfield's conception of the Ohio country as an ideological battleground between two forces—the Jeffersonian ideal of the yeoman farmer versus the destructive Hamiltonian philosophy of trade and industry. Three passages describe the transition of the region from pristine wilderness into industrial wasteland. A stream called Toby's Run, viewed by the owner, flows clear among wooded hills, although its corruption has begun: the name derives from a native dweller who drowned there, drunk on the whiskey the settlers brought. Next the stream is described through the consciousness of the pioneer's son-in-law just before the outbreak of the Civil War. The hills, denuded of trees, are covered by houses, and although the waters are still clear, cinders and gravel have begun to fall from the railroad bridge that now spans it. Finally, the founder's great-grandson, at the outbreak of the Great War, gazes at the stream that has become a sewer carrying debris and pollution from the factories to the river. Houses along the stream are not pioneers' cabins but hovels, where factory workers live in conditions as degraded as the river. The name Toby's Run remains, however, underscoring the beginnings of the corruption of the wilderness, although the townspeople have forgotten its origin as well as its history.

Whereas his novels tell of alienation and disruption, Bromfield's seven volumes of nonfiction, written in his last fifteen years, demonstrate the way toward belonging and fulfillment, not in the pursuit of material success but in learning to live in harmony with nature. Those works are *Pleasant Valley* (1945), his account of the return to Ohio and the first six years of his experiment in sustainable agriculture; *A Few Brass Tacks* (1946), a study of economic imbalances and their possible remedy in strong communities; *Malabar Farm* (1948), the record of his observations and experiments, together with an account of his successes and failures; *Out of the Earth* (1950), almost an agricultural textbook on restoring soil; *A New Pattern for a Tired World* (1954), his most ambitious socioeconomic work; *From My Experience* (1955), a reappraisal of his work on the farm; and *Animals and Other People* (1955), a collection of his best nonfiction essays.

The story of Bromfield's return to Ohio and farming begins with a trip Louis and Mary took to France in 1924, which turned out to be a stay of fourteen years. The Bromfields leased a house with a large garden in Senlis near Paris where Louis wrote and fulfilled his passion for gardening. They entertained a diverse group of people from nobility to peasants, on Sundays receiving as many as eighty guests, which included F. Scott and Zelda Fitzgerald, Somerset Maugham, Edith Wharton, Edna Ferber, Pablo Picasso, and the Maharajah of Baroda. Bromfield wrote later in *Malabar Farm* that one of the most stimulating of his wide acquaintance was Gertrude Stein; he described her as naturally brilliant and praised her immense capacity for enjoyment of the moment. Although Bromfield traveled widely—in Spain, England, Cornwall, Switzerland, Denmark, Austria, Holland, Indonesia, and India—he was most attracted to France: if fortune smiled, the French knew how to spend their money; if not, they knew how to make the best of a bad situation. In *Pleasant Valley* Bromfield includes this tribute: "I am deeply grateful to the French for what I learned from them of the earth, of human values and dignity and decency and reality. And I am grateful to Louis Gillet, dead now of a heart broken by the humiliation of France, for the long talk of the evening in the moonlit forest of Ermenonville while we listened to the calling of the amorous stags, for he sent me back to the country where I was born, to Pleasant Valley and the richest life I have ever known." The Bromfields left France reluctantly when the next war became imminent and Louis was convinced that he could help his adopted country more from within the United States.

Louis had been contemplating the idea of buying a farm in the United States before 1933 while writing The Farm. The family, which by then included three daughters, returned before him in 1938 while he remained to help with war relief in the Spanish Civil War. The following year he bought three adjoining farms in Richland County, Ohio, and the family set out on the way of life that was to occupy them until Louis's death. Thomas Wolfe notwithstanding, Louis did go home again. The farms—the Anson, Fleming, and Ferguson places—described in Pleasant Valley included one thousand acres which had at one time all belonged to John Ferguson, a hunter and trapper who had been given a deed of 640 acres of forest by President James Monroe, and whose family line ended in 1890. In the pile of deeds, writes Bromfield the novelist, lay the human history of the place—of marriages, births and deaths, quarrels, bargaining and bankruptcies, and strange tales like that of Ceely Rose, the miller's daughter, who murdered her parents because (she thought) they would not let her marry the man she loved.

The story, however, was not recorded only on paper but in the earth, forests, and buildings; it also constituted "a sad history of rich land slipping downhill over a period of more than a century. The story was sadder even than the history of the births and deaths, the crimes and the murders written into the deeds. It was the story of good earth being murdered by carelessness and bad farming and greed and ignorance." Bromfield describes his three reasons for choosing Pleasant Valley as his location: he had loved the valley and had never really been able to escape it; he could not tolerate the thought of living where the land was completely flat; and he wanted to prove that worn-out farms could be restored and that hill country could be farmed successfully. He explains the deeper reason for undertaking his experiment:

> I knew in my heart that we as a nation were already much farther along the path to destruction than most people knew. What we needed was a new kind of pioneer, not the sort which cut down the forests and burned off the prairies and raped the land, but pioneers who created new forests and healed and restored the richness of the country God had given us, that richness which, from the moment the first settler landed on the Atlantic coast we had done our best to destroy. I had a foolish idea that I wanted to be one of that new race of pioneers.

Here Bromfield joins ranks with Aldo Leopold, Wendell Berry, Gary Snyder, and Wes Jackson in proposing a new way of life drawn from tradition but inspired by a new ecological ethos.

The Great House at Malabar Farm (named for the Malabar Coast of India), however, did not resemble a pioneer's cabin. Bromfield wanted it to represent the New England architectural style that he thought characterized northern Ohio, arguing that architecture should be suited to place and way of life. The dormer windows imitated the style of the inn at Zoar, a nineteenth century communal agricultural experiment founded in Tuscarawas County by German settlers. Craftsmen as skilled and careful as those Bromfield had known in Europe created the cabinetry and woodwork. The twin stairways and big doorways at either end of the big hall combined the simplicity and dignity of the Jeffersonian Greek Revival style. Purposely designed to look as if it had been added onto, the house was intended to be put to hard use. Not only was Malabar a working farm but also the scene of much coming and going. The Bromfields remained social people who were well liked and sought after as they had been in France, and Louis wrote in *Malabar Farm* that scarcely a week passed "without visitors from some remote part of the world as well as from all parts of the United States." Describing the vista from the house, Bromfield explains the importance of landscape and memory:

> It stands overlooking the Valley which I loved as a boy and still love better than any valley in the world. I fished the creek below and ranged the hills and woods hunting and gathering nuts as a small boy. I swam in the swimming hole where now the kids of the farm go swimming. I find there the continuity which existed in France, that growing of one thing into another, the succession of generation by generation, which is the rich, satisfying rule of Nature herself and indeed of all civilization. I think the dream of that house was there long ago in the days when as a small boy I knew every tree and spring and pasture in the Valley.

Bromfield sounds prophetic when he foresees the time when his house would receive visitors as a state park: "Perhaps one day it will belong to the state together with the hills, valleys and woods of Malabar Farm."

Like Aldo Leopold, Bromfield believed a farm was the best teacher. He begins chapter 11 of *Pleasant Valley* with the Confucian saying that "The best fertilizer on any farm is the footsteps of the owner." In an acre, Bromfield asserts, there is the whole of the universe and the answer to most of man's problems. He held good farmers to be among the most intelligent citizens and among the best educated people because they had to know more than any other professionals: "A good farmer must be many things—a horticulturist, a mechanic, a botanist, an ecologist, a veterinary, a biologist and any number of other things—but knowledge is not enough. There must be too that *feel* of all with which nature concerns herself." Agriculture was the most satisfactory and inexhaustible of the sciences because it included so many other areas of study. The good farmer knew and appreciated tradition but also kept an open mind, ready to absorb new ideas, and therefore he was a stimulating conversationalist and companion.

Even so, the knowledge was being forgotten, as many farmers in America used up the soil until it was worthless and left the area. Exceptions to this pattern were the Pennsylvania Dutch, the Amish, and the Mennonites who lived closely among themselves. Farmers whose ancestors had immigrated long ago turned out to be poorer farmers than the more recent arrivals, Bromfield observed, because older European methods of farming were unsuitable to the American soil and climate. The more recent immigrant farmers, however, had learned from scarcity that they must conserve, and this experience put them ahead of the farmers whose families had long been in America.

Slowly a system of sustainable agriculture suitable to the United States had evolved, not primarily from Europe but from Asia and the Near East, of using terraced crops, cover crops, proper drainage and forestry, natural fertilizer, diversified planting, and crop rotation. Writing only fifteen years after the Dust Bowl, Bromfield advised readers that America is not a land of limitless resources and that the American method of "mining" the soil for its fertility had become bankrupt. One of Bromfield's suggestions was that farmers learn from garden clubs, to which he gave many lectures, because gardeners often knew more about soil.

Sounding very contemporary, Bromfield lamented that the sickness of American agriculture was due in part to the gradual disappearance of the family farm and its replacement with mechanized farms more like industries. He did not believe that the impulse of the time toward regimentation, centralization, mechanization, and industrialism represented true progress; instead, they produced material rewards at the cost of human stamina, decency, and dignity. He lamented that the high cost of machinery prevented young people from going into farming, much as the high cost of land prevents many from pursuing farming today. Modern economics thus subverted the dream of the self-contained family farm, which Bromfield believed represented the heart of social harmony.

Bromfield echoes Henry David Thoreau and precedes Wendell Berry when he states that a nation is based on its natural resources, forests, and agriculture. In the preface to *Pleasant Valley*, he writes that "agriculture is the keystone of our economic structure" and "the wealth, welfare, prosperity and even the future freedom of this nation are based upon the soil." The nation was beginning to pay for the destruction its greed had brought, Bromfield warned. A tremendous job of restoration and reconstruction awaited the country, greater than the job of subduing the wilderness. Later in the book Bromfield sounds again his call for a new type of pioneer farmer:

> What we need is a new courage and a new race of pioneers, as sturdy as the original pioneers, but wiser than they—a race of pioneers concerned with the physical, economic and social paradise which this country could be. . . . These new pioneers will have to be men who sit not in libraries working out theories, but men who understand the people of this country and the illimitable wealth of its natural resources and beauties, and above all the fact that there is wealth for all and a good life and that it is founded, as is the wealth and well-being of every sound nation, upon its soil, its water and its forest.

When the soil was gone, the nation would be gone, even "its crude materialistic and mechanical manifestations." Short of war, there was no greater human folly than allowing soil erosion. In *Malabar Farm* Bromfield continues this theme:

> Out of the earth we came and to the earth we return, and it is the earth itself which determines largely our health, our longevity, our vigor, even our character. In the broadest sense any nation is as vigorous and as powerful as its natural resources, and among them the most important are agriculture and forests, for these

are eternally renewable and productive if managed properly. Upon them, and largely upon agriculture depends another vast source of any nation's power—the health, vigor, intelligence and ingenuity of its citizens.

When agriculture fades, the civilization fades; therefore, permitting the soil to erode constituted moral failure. "Man himself cannot escape from Nature," Bromfield writes in *Pleasant Valley*, "Neither can he ever subdue her or attempt to exploit her endlessly without becoming himself the victim." In *Malabar Farm* he continues, "Nature is still unconquered by man and when he attempts to upset or circumvent her laws, he merely courts disaster, misery, low living standards, and eventual destruction." His statements seem especially far reaching in this time when climate change, caused by burning fossil fuels, presents our greatest challenge.

Bromfield also articulated a new economics based on longterm investment in the land and people. There would be no shortcut through socialism, communism, capitalism, or fascism. Marxism, with its emphasis on materialism, negated all that man is; however, wrote Bromfield presciently, those who believed that industry and technology were the sole means of liberation were as wrong as the Marxists. Neither the boom businessman nor the New Dealer understood that theories would not make a strong culture: good farming communities, however, could create economic security. The American nation had every possible advantage with rich resources and freedom from invasions, but it had the mentality of the rich son who wastes what he inherits, Bromfield continues in *Pleasant Valley*. Theodore Roosevelt and Gifford Pinchot knew that in a democracy action must come from the people and not be imposed on them, but the government should invest heavily in education so that people could understand the choices before them. Industry and great cities brought the evil of economic insecurity, Bromfield wrote in *Malabar Farm*; like Robinson Jeffers in "Shine, Perishing Republic," Bromfield foresaw a period of decline for the United States: "Sometimes it seems to me that we are in a period resembling the beginning of the disintegration of the Roman Empire, one of those periods when 'civilization' having reached a peak, starts slipping back again out of sheer weariness and moral decadence through a kind of anarchy into a simplified primitive existence."

For an example of the best kind of life, Bromfield goes again to the French. The permanence and continuity of the French culture had emanated from its contact with the soil. The French peasant or working man had a little plot of ground and modest house and wages but had more permanence and stability than the American worker or even white-collar businessman who received higher wages but who rented his house and was perpetually in debt for his car, radio, and other luxuries. The so-called high standard of living of Americans was an illusion, based on credit and installment payments, which caused homelessness and penury if the husband lost his job. Bromfield continued in *Pleasant Valley* that "real continuity, real love of one's country, real permanence had to do not with mechanical inventions and high wages but with the earth and man's love of the soil upon which he lived." What Bromfield missed most about France, he wrote, was not the intellectual life or the "curious special freedom" a foreigner feels in a country he or she knows well, but the old house and few acres that he had worked for fourteen years. Of all his honors he especially valued the diploma given him by the Workingmen-Gardeners' Association of France for his skill as a gardener and the medal given him by the Ministry of Agriculture for introducing American vegetables into popular cultivation in the market garden area surrounding the city of Paris. He tells the story of his friend Bosquet who had a few acres on which he grew virtually every sort of vegetable; kept chickens, ducks, pigs, and goats; built his own house with help from friends; and owned everything he had—house, furniture, old car, gramophone, records. He worked in a machine-tool factory. When he was laid off, he and his family never went hungry because they grew everything they ate. Manure from the livestock went back into the soil as fertilizer. He gathered fuel from the nearby state-owned forest. This life Bromfield contrasts with that of the laid-off American worker who was in debt for everything and who went on relief when unemployed. The Depression, Bromfield explains, stemmed from American extravagance and the conviction that there is always more to exploit. The whole society has convinced the worker that it was his patriotic duty to buy as much as possible on the installment plan. The laws of economics are as immutable as the laws of nature and mathematics, however, and so if costs are not recovered, the whole enterprise collapses. Sounding like Aldo Leopold, he continues in *Malabar Farm* that material things are not what provide security or happiness:

> One might add that all this is true and that it might save the world if the trill from a migrating sparrow could be heard above the clamor for higher wages, higher profits, election promises, water closets and automobiles, above all the outcry for materialist things and standards by which man does *not* live, by which eventually he dies the death of the soul, of the spirit, of all understanding and growth, in the end, of decency itself. An age in which God is represented by the Holy Trinity of plumbing, overtime and assembly lines is not a great age, unless man learns to use these things for his freedom and the growth of his spirit rather than his brutalization.

Bromfield's religious views—like Leopold's, Jeffers's, Berry's, and Snyder's—are centered in the relationship to nature, not in transcending it. In *Pleasant Valley* he writes that living close to wild creatures enabled him to feel an integral part of the grandeur and beauty of nature and to understand the beliefs of the Jains of India who believed that lives, even those of insects, were sacred. Religion never came to him through churches or people but by seeing "the beautiful dignity of the small animals of the field, of a fern growing from a damp crevice in the rock, or a tulip tree rising straight and clean a hundred feet toward the sky." Many of the best farmers were not regular churchgoers or religious in the conventional sense because their faith arose not from a church or creed but from closeness to the land.

The otherwise bucolic narrative of *Malabar Farm* includes a tale of heroism arising from the French Resistance. Denyse Clairouin, whom the Bromfields had known in France, visited Malabar Farm in 1941 on a visa secured for her by someone working for the Underground inside the Vichy government. Through her and his French publisher, Louis donated all his royalties to the Underground, a transaction which could not have occurred except between two French citizens. His royalties otherwise would have been seized by the Germans who prohibited the publication of his books after they occupied France and who had long since proscribed his writings in Germany.

Clairouin was arrested, however, after her return to France and died in Mauthausen concentration camp in 1945. Thus does Bromfield show that no place, however rural, can ever be entirely separated from the rest of the world politically as well as ecologically.

Bromfield's patriotism nevertheless escaped officials in the United States. The *Mansfield News Journal* revealed on August 22, 1999, that the FBI had kept a file on him between 1941 and 1954, including information on his speeches and social affiliations. Among his most suspicious activities, the report states, were the facts that he was living on a large farm where he entertained an unusually large number of visitors—some of whom were under FBI surveillance; gave Sunday sermons on farming techniques and soil conservation; and knew and socialized with many Hollywood stars. The file included the information that Bromfield was interested in Russia and France and that he had lived outside the country for a long time. Also causing suspicion was a letter he had written saying that he would be a sponsor for the Committee for the Protection of the Foreign Born, which fought an attempt to deprive a California resident and Communist Party member of his naturalized citizenship. A memo dated June 9, 1943, and published in 1999 by the *News Journal* reveals the extent of the FBI's knowledge:

Bromfield still residing at Malabar Farm, Lucas, Ohio; follows the occupation of gentleman farmer and writes weekly syndicated newspaper column entitled "Voice from the Country." In this column he acts as spokesman for the farmers and discusses various political and economic problems of current interest. Has been visited by [name blacked out] Managing Editor of the Daily Worker, and [name blacked out] Ohio State Communist Party Secretary. He is reported interested in work of Joint Anti-Fascist Refugee Committee, an alleged Communist Front; was a sponsor for American Soviet Friendship Rally in Cleveland, Ohio; and spoke at Chicago meeting of "France Forever," criticizing United States policy in North Africa and recommending post-war alliance between United States and Russia as basis for a stable post-war arrangement.

The file ends with a two-page memo dated May 28, 1954, which includes four paragraphs of Bromfield's alleged affiliations and activities and concludes that he was a "communist sympathizer." The agent probably had not read Bromfield's books on farming, however, for the file does not include his assertion in Pleasant Valley that the design of Malabar Farm was based on a Russian commune and in Malabar Farm that the success of reactionary politics was always checked by its own smugness and capacity for underestimating other people. Whatever their motivation for the investigation, the FBI did not stop Bromfield's work.

Pleasant Valley and Malabar Farm stand as elegant testimonies to faith in the earth. The lyrical opening of Malabar Farm signals the reader to the descriptions of the cycles of nature to follow: "August 31 [1944]: The drought broke today with a heavy, slow, soaking rain which began during the night and continued all through the day. Forty-six days without rain, save one or two thunderstorms, has left the corn that was planted early in the season parched and dry with only undeveloped nubbins as ears. . . . Drought in our green Ohio country where it is seldom expected is a shocking experience. It raises in good Ohioans a sense of indignation and outrage." The book is a collection of diverse pieces, five of seventeen being journals of a farm year representing the four seasons (with two summer journals), discussions of Bromfield's philosophy of farming, chapters on new farming methods, the life cycle of a farm pond, and grass as healer for soil deprived of humus. In its tapestry of descriptions of farm practice, wildlife, economic theory based on soil conservation, and cultural theory based on small communities, *Malabar Farm* reads like a forerunner of Snyder's *The Practice of the Wild*.

Malabar Farm and *Pleasant Valley* are narrations of hope as the farm itself is a working monument to that hope. Families visit the Great House and hear about the writer's movie star friends who helped with weeding and canning. They also tour the barns and fields and learn about experimental agricultural practices—crop and grazing rotation, contour farming, composting—which have become widespread due to the influence of environmentalists and visionaries like Bromfield.

Chapter Eleven

A Gift to Be Simple

A 2003 STUDY by the Ohio State University's agricultural extension service in Geauga County revealed that the net profit per acre for Amish wheat farmers was $126 while for conventional farmers it was $10. The study went on to show that start-up and operational costs for the Amish farmers were about 5 percent of what they were for conventional farmers, one reason being that labor costs are much lower for Amish farmers whose children do much of the work. Another is that their farms, averaging 60 acres, are smaller and more easily worked with horse-drawn equipment than larger farms averaging 500 to 1,000 acres and often worked by only one or two people. Many Amish children, who leave school at the end of eighth grade, work throughout their adolescence on the farm while others go to work in factories and restaurants but turn over their wages to their parents. Most Amish live at home until they marry, so grown sons and daughters continue to help the family.

They call themselves "the plain people," and simplicity is what they say they desire. The children go barefoot in all seasons except winter. Clothing conforms to the practices of the church: men wear denim overalls and hats; women long dresses, aprons, and bonnets. Some more liberal Amish groups allow men to wear straw hats and women to wear green, purple, or blue dresses and white caps. Their houses have no electricity, they use horse-drawn buggies and wagons for travel, and they do not serve in the armed forces. Most do not vote, although some do. The church began in the seventeenth century in Switzerland when their group, named for Jakob Ammann, broke from the Swiss Brethren, part of the Anabaptist Movement begun by liberal Protestants who wanted to eliminate all vestiges of Catholic practice from their churches. The Anabaptists eventually divided into three groups—Brethren, Mennonites (named for the Dutch priest Menno Simons), and Amish—whose differences with the others stemmed not from belief but practice. All Anabaptists were persecuted by Catholics and more conservative Protestant groups, causing them to move to the hinterlands and take up farming for their livelihood. Eventually the Dutch Mennonites were tolerated, while the Swiss Brethren were persecuted for centuries. Large numbers immigrated to other countries, particularly the United States. The largest Amish settlement in the world, numbering over two hundred thousand, is in Holmes County, Ohio, and many live in the surrounding counties of Wayne, Ashland, Richland, Knox, and Tuscarawas. There are sizable communities in Pennsylvania, Indiana, Illinois, Wisconsin, Kentucky, and other states and countries, including Canada and Belize.

In America, both Brethren and Amish broke into smaller groups, the Brethren splitting into the Church of the Brethren, which remained pacifist, and the Brethren Church, which abandoned pacifism after the Second World War. The Amish divided themselves into even more groups, each based on practice— what kind of clothing they wear, what color buggy they drive, or whether they worship at home or in church. There are "wide-brim Amish" and "narrow-brim Amish"; "black-hat Amish" and "straw-hat Amish"; "black-buggy Amish" and "yellow-buggy Amish"; "house Amish" (the most conservative) and "church Amish." Just as many non-Amish mistakenly believe that all Amish belong to one order, the Amish refer to those outside their community by all-encompassing terms—*anner Satt leit* ("the other kind of people"), or "the English." Even recent immigrants from Mexico or Asia are called "the English."

What unites the Amish is their literal interpretation of the New Testament injunction of separation from the world, especially Romans 12:2 ("Be not conformed to this world: but be ye transformed by the renewing of your mind that ye may prove what is that good, and acceptable, and perfect, will of God") and II Corinthians 6:14 ("Be ye not unequally yoked together with unbelievers: for what fellowship hath righteousness with unrighteousness?"). They base their pacifism on John 18:36: "My kingdom is not of this world: if my kingdom were of this world, then would my servants fight." Even their philosophy of life, seemingly so attached to the earth, is otherworldly: they view themselves as "strangers and pilgrims" in the present and emphasize obedience and self-denial over the notion of "grace by faith alone" as some Protestant groups do. None knows until the Judgement Day of his or her salvation. One of the greatest of all sins is that of pride, either of knowledge or personal display. Weddings are simple affairs, usually with no names attached to wedding gifts. Photographs are forbidden as evidence of vanity. Some Amish believe that even keeping themselves, their children, or their farms clean is evidence of the sin of pride, while others believe that cleanliness is their duty, and so many non-Amish neighbors incorrectly distinguish between only two types, the "dirty" and the "clean" Amish.

One controversy between Amish and Mennonites included the practices of shunning those who departed from Amish custom and excommunicating women who spoke falsehoods, and the conviction that noble-hearted non-Amish people could be saved. Believing that one's own sect had the only answer to salvation was nothing new, of course; what was different was that they did not seek converts, preferring to bring new members to the church only through their own families. The most liberal of the Anabaptist sects had become the most conservative.

The Amish are indeed resourceful. They know how to grow food, build houses, and install plumbing. They are all trilingual, speaking their own dialect of German, High German, and English. Amish communities have survived and grown, while the Shakers (who did not believe in procreation but depended on conversion for membership), Mennonites of the Zoar community, and the followers of Fourier (Brook Farm, Massachusetts) and Owen (New Harmony, Indiana) did not. They keep in touch: their newspaper, The Budget, published (in English) in Walnut Creek, Ohio, contains information about Amish families as far away as Pennsylvania and Wisconsin.

They are a visible part of the larger community: one sees hitching posts at nearly every large store and hospital in Ashland, Wayne, and Holmes Counties. The large medical facility of the Cleveland Clinic in Wooster set aside an area of its parking lot for buggies. One Thanksgiving day, during a drive through Millersburg—the town called the "heart" of the Amish country—I saw more buggies than cars. On a recent farm tour visit in Tuscarawas County, I encountered more buggies than cars, partly because it was Sunday, which they set aside for visiting. Many families supplement farm income by selling storage sheds and birdhouses. A common sight along the roads in Amish country is a buggy and a family selling commodities—handwoven rugs, scarves, birdhouses, bread, pies, and jam—while the tethered horse grazes beside them. The Amish always had more and better produce than I did when years ago I sold some of my crop at the local auction, and so I gave up raising produce for sale. Driving Route 96 between Ashland and Mansfield, one can see Amish children playing on swings and a slide in the yard of a one-room schoolhouse. Horses wait patiently in a stable outside a Mennonite church on a narrow road in Clear Creek Township in northern Ashland County while parishioners worship on Sunday in a church that has no windows—so no curious onlookers can disturb them.

David Kline, an Amish man who has lived and worked on the same seventy-acre family farm in north-central Ohio for over fifty years, is also the author of two books, *Great Possessions: An Amish Farmer's Journal* and *Scratching the Woodchuck: Nature on an Amish Farm*, and for a long time edited the magazine *Farming, People, Land, and Community*. The first is structured, like Aldo Leopold's *A Sand County Almanac* (which was also to have been titled "Great Possessions") and Bromfield's *Malabar Farm*, according to the seasons. Kline describes primarily the bird life he is able to attract to his farm in Holmes County because he practices diversified agriculture. He also describes other wildlife such as deer and insects and devotes a chapter to the American chestnut. As Aldo Leopold names a chapter for the band number of a chickadee, Kline names one for the band number of a Canada goose. His brief introduction includes his philosophy: "The Amish are not necessarily against modern technology," he writes; "We have simply chosen not to be controlled by it." He describes a neighbor who used chemicals to kill weeds in accordance with the no-till technology, which is supposed to save farmers time and help to conserve soil, but which killed off nesting bobolinks. In *Great Possessions* Kline laments the loss that farmers will sustain who are eager to ease the burden of their work with the chemicals required by no-till: "Presently no-till farming with its dependence on vast amounts of chemicals is being touted by the experts as the way to guarantee green fields forever. What they fail to say is that those green fields will be strangely silent—gone will be the bobolink, the meadowlark, and the sweet song of the vesper sparrow in the twilight."

Kline emphasizes the type of crop rotation that discourages insects and thus eliminates the need for insecticides. When corn follows hay, he advises, there are fewer crop-damaging insects. He paraphrases Wes Jackson on what is often described as the tedium of farming: "The pleasantness or unpleasantness of farm work depends upon the scale—upon the size of the field and the size of the crop." By staying with the horse, the Amish have maintained a proper scale, says Kline. With farms the size of his, there is always something to do, yet farmers are not overwhelmed. Families work together and thereby grow together. While doing chores with his son, Kline was able to hear about the issues of adolescence. When he, his wife, and five of their children bundled straw on a thirteen-acre wheat field (a chore called "shocking"), the job was soon finished because everyone helped.

Kline's Amish upbringing does not seem to have limited his acquaintance with the world. He writes knowledgeably not only of farming practices but also wildlife and geology. In *Great Possessions* he includes a detailed history of three alien species intentionally introduced which are considered by many to have become pests—the starling, house sparrow, and carp. He states that Hotspur's line in *I Henry IV* about starlings led to their being brought to America: "Nay, I'll have a starling shall be taught to speak / nothing but 'Mortimer.'" The breadth of Kline's knowledge seems to disprove the commonly held assumption that the Amish are barely literate because they leave school after the eighth grade: it was drug manufacturer Eugene Schieffelin who introduced a hundred starlings into Central Park in New York City merely because he wanted all birds mentioned in Shakespeare's works to be present in the United States. (They may be considered pests, but flocking starlings weave beautiful patterns over the fields in autumn.)

The desire to live simply is not new: Ben Jonson praised the virtues of Penshurst; the Romantics sought a more honest and liberating way of life; Thomas Jefferson declared that his new nation should be one of yeoman farmers; idealistic young people created a back-to-the-land movement in the 1960s. Antiquarianism is also not new: most societies have a form of the belief that somewhere and at some time, people lived simpler, nobler, more meaningful lives, whether in a golden age of the past or a more primitive place in contemporary times. It is understandable that people romanticize a culture based on strong family values, self-sufficiency, and identification with place. Pictures of Amish farms and buggies decorate calendars, and people look to the

Amish example for evidence of the strength of community. Residents of this area enjoy the musical sound of shod horse hooves on pavement and the sight of buggies along the sides of roads.

We often frame our vision, however, to suit our ideals. The workmen who built Penshurst and the servants who labored there lived in a stratified society that offered them few choices; the Romantics, like the sixties generation after them, found themselves irrevocably part of the culture they wished to leave; the yeoman farmers of America found it difficult or impossible to compete with large plantation owners, even as farm families now find it difficult or impossible to compete with agribusiness. Although diversified farming helps to protect ecosystems, and Amish separation from the world necessitates admirable self-reliance, they employ modern conveniences, and they sometimes hold their communities together by coercion, not cooperation.

As a child I visited many Amish farms with my father, and for a time I envied their way of life. After moving to Ashland County, I observed more closely. I knew that they live, work, and trade with non-Amish, but I did not know the extent to which they use modern products and equipment. My first surprise was in seeing them in the grocery stores in Loudonville buying items like frozen pizza and ice cream, which they pack into Coleman containers for the ride home. They cannot own cars or telephones, but they can rent them: many communities before the age of cell phones installed coin-operated telephones for community use.

Anyone expecting Amish workers to build the old way will be disappointed. When I hired a fencing company from Sugar Creek, four Amish men showed up. The post pounder and chain saws were completely modern, but they were leased, not owned, by the company. (This practice of leasing leads non-Amish to describe them as "sneaky," an epithet that could be attached to any religious group that does not adhere literally to its own teachings.) Far from making all their own clothes, the Amish sometimes shop in clothing stores. While the women do make most of their dresses, many of the men's bib overalls come from China. One day in the very large Meijer store in Mansfield

I saw many Amish. Outside, a Greyhound touring bus, hired for that day, waited while dozens of bonneted women loaded their purchases into the luggage hold. They sometimes rent smaller vans to shop in the stores in Loudonville and Ashland.

Young Amish men and women may listen to popular music, even rock music, so long as they have not yet married or joined the church, which they do at age twenty-one. Young men used to carry boom boxes or radios in the backs of their buggies; now they have MP3 players. Likewise, the belief that their way of life is quiet and pleasant is not entirely accurate. While they don't have electric tools, they have gas-driven machines that are sometimes ear-splittingly loud. I take my horse tack to a leather worker who uses a noisy gas-powered cutter. Some neighbors have told me they once lived beside an Amish family that operated their own sawmill: from dawn to dusk the ripsaws roared, shattering the peace and quiet of the countryside. No laws could be invoked to stop it because the area was zoned for general farm use, which allows family-run businesses.

The image of the entire Amish family working only on the farm is misleading. Unmarried girls serve as waitresses in the restaurants in the Holmes County towns of Millersburg, Sugar Creek, Walnut Creek, and Berlin. An Amish grocery store in Loudonville does a brisk business in homegrown produce, homemade cheese, and home-baked pastries. Many boys go to work in local cheese factories and lumber mills. A company need have only one Amish worker in order to claim that its products are "Amish made." Some Amish men hire themselves out as carpenters and even electricians because there are no licensing requirements outside incorporated towns. Self-taught Amish electricians and plumbers are not always competent, as we learned when we had to have nearly everything in our own house replaced or repaired that had been installed by Amish workers. Their honesty and craftsmanship are highly rated, but, like people everywhere, not all are skilled, and not all are honest. The Amish respect for the land does not always apply to the rest of the world; I have seen Amish at the local hay auction and fair throw paper plates and napkins onto the ground even when trash bins were close, although I hope these people do not represent the majority of their group.

The Amish are mostly law-abiding and community oriented, but they do not like to become involved with the "English" even if their own best interests are at stake. They do not regularly take part in task forces that monitor zoning changes or groups that seek to protect waterways and parks. While some Amish leave the church, very few people ever join because the rules of membership keep their communities closed to almost everyone not born into them. When a colleague tried to become a member of an Amish church, the elders told him he would first have to leave his wife and four children because he had been married before. He declined.

The Amish way of life is more sustainable than that of the larger culture because the community members produce much of what they consume, yet like non-Amish they consume things they do not produce, including conveniences that create waste, such as disposable containers. They also find land scarce. Although about 10 percent of their number leave the Amish way of life when they turn eighteen, their numbers are growing because they have large families (ten to fifteen children are not uncommon) and many try to purchase land from non-Amish. When they buy "English" houses they tear out the electrical wiring but retain other conveniences. In Holmes County I have seen bonneted women sitting on plastic Walmart chairs on the decks of split-level houses.

A young woman of my acquaintance who left her Amish family told me that she realized very early that she would leave the community, but she had to keep quiet about her plans right up until her eighteenth birthday. She worked in a factory after she finished eighth grade and turned all her wages over to her father who never explained to her how he used the money. Child labor laws do not apply to their situation, as parents in most states have the option of taking their children's earnings until age eighteen. She did what most Amish do who want to leave the order—she made friends with an "English" woman who gave her a home until she could save enough money to finish her GED and enroll in college. Choosing the larger world often means separation from families. Many who leave know they cannot return, even to visit. Although she had not officially joined the church before she left home, my acquaintance had not seen her parents or siblings for four years.

This young woman and others who have left the Amish tell me that, far from the simple life where everyone is equal and people help each other, Amish communities have the same stratification the larger society has. The families with least prestige are those in which one or the other parent suffers from some mental illness—more common among the Amish than outsiders know. While they will consult physicians, they will never go to psychiatrists or psychologists because they believe that mental illness stems from personal failure. Clinical depression thus has the status of a character flaw, and the whole family suffers from discrimination by the rest of the community. It is true that when one family needs help—getting in a harvest, for example, or rebuilding a barn that has burned down—the whole community shows up to pitch in. They then return home, my acquaintances tell me, to gossip about the family who was careless enough to let the barn catch fire.

A common belief among Amish women is that having large numbers of children will give them a better place in heaven, and they compete with each other to see who can have the most. Death of infants or children is considered the mother's failure. One former Amish woman told me about a mother who bragged widely about her eight healthy children but suffered a nervous breakdown when her ninth child died. She grieved, my acquaintance claimed, not because her son was dead but because she believed the death was her fault. Amish women view postnatal depression as a moral failure because they revile no one more than a woman who is not thrilled to have a new baby. My acquaintance described bright-eyed young women who married and set up housekeeping only to find a few years or even months later that they had tied themselves to lives of grinding drudgery. Once a woman has children, she finds it impossible to leave them or support herself, for she has no marketable skills other than domestic labor. Although the Amish way of life involves strict stratification of authority with the men running the farm and women caring for the house, children, and garden, many people believe there is much equality between men and women; however, the men have all the power in decisions about the family and the community. The women do rule the house, but that is the only place where they have any influence. The story of the assault and beard cutting by members of an Amish breakaway sect at Bergholz, Ohio, in 2012 made national headlines, but not so for another true crime story that involved an Amish husband in Wayne County and his girlfriend (a married Mennonite woman) who murdered his wife so that he could be free without having to leave the church.

The most stifling part of the Amish upbringing, however, is not the rules about dress or conduct or even the gossip of neighbors; it is that children are often taught not to ask questions about belief or practice. When they do, the most common answer is "because we do it that way," whether the query involves clothing, farm practice, or theology. My acquaintance had never been praised for her intelligence and never even realized that she was a quick learner, as most Amish do not prize reading, writing, and learning other than knowledge of farm practices. Any child who shows curiosity realizes quickly not to try to elicit answers from an Amish person but to wait until he or she can have contact with "the English." Amish children learn to distrust each other because they never know who will report "worldly" questions to parents or clergy, as people who lived under totalitarian regimes say that they had to be extremely careful whom they trusted.

There are many happy Amish people, however, and there is much to recommend their way of life. A former Amish man of my acquaintance says that he never experienced ostracism or shunning when he left home at twenty-six to marry a non-Amish woman whom his family accepted completely. He explained that he had never joined the church and so did not have to upset the family by leaving it, but he also knew people who had left the church after having joined and were still not shunned by their families, who adopted a more accepting attitude toward those who left. A former colleague of mine who lives near Amish farms told me the young Amish women in the community threw a large party to honor the older people—non-Amish and Amish alike. Most significantly for me is the fact that Amish farming impacts the environment far less than conventional practices. The Amish, furthermore, seem to be the only people who have found a way to circumvent agribusiness, which prevents anyone who is not independently wealthy or who does not inherit land from farming.

Rural electrification in the 1930s was considered a great innovation, but ubiquitous power derived from fossil fuel has compromised our independence and self-reliance. I prefer washing clothes by hand, hanging them up to dry, and pumping water from a well and would like to keep food in a root cellar rather than a refrigerator. Most of all I would like to do away with the noise of motor vehicles and return to the quiet music of horse hooves on pavement. We think we travel farther and faster with the internal combustion engine, but I am not sure that is the case, as we also spend a great deal of time in traffic jams.

Watching Amish horses trotting down the city streets or country roads, I consider that the route to freedom is not fewer choices but more, including the flexibility to realize higher ideals rather than our present situation in which a few influential, wealthy people decide how the rest will live. My belief in traditionalism and sustainability, however, coincides with a belief in the importance of questioning the status quo, as Jakob Amman did two centuries ago. I would certainly like to reverse dependence on fossil fuel, pollution of air and water, and suburbanization, which are some of the banes of the last century, but I would not want to jeopardize the civil rights and women's emancipation that are also its gifts.

Our failures as much as our successes give us our energy, our need for art, and our desire to strive for change but also to preserve what we love. Morality should not be defined by divine retribution but by engagement with the world and acceptance of responsibility for actions. Sustainable land use and modes of transportation as well as more choices of livelihood could enable people to create a better society than imagining an elusive paradise that has never existed.

Chapter Twelve

A Tale Better Told in the Retelling

I HAVE KNOWN several people who tried to put Wes Jackson's and Louis Bromfield's ideas into practice, becoming pioneer farmers and homesteaders. One friend moved with her husband, brother-in-law, and his wife to California where they built their own house and grew their own food on a mountainside north of Eureka. The front of their house was pointed like a ship's prow forging its way not through waves but through branches of tan oak and sequoia. In 1998 at the annual Horse Progress Days event in Holmes County, I met a young man who had been raised in the late seventies on a commune by hippie parents and who started his own farm in the Maryland hills. For years during the 1970s, when I went hiking in the Wayne National Forest, I passed a small, old-fashioned trailer that stood on a hillside. A proud sign read "Oleo Acres—a Cheap Spread."

One of the most interesting stories of self-sufficiency, however, came from an academic colleague. When President Johnson unveiled his Great Society program in 1964, some people claimed that subsistence farmers in Appalachia and the rural South were poor because they were uneducated; others declared that laziness accounted for their poverty. On the contrary, "I thought it looked like a great way to live," Elliot Gaines said. Raised in suburban New Jersey, the son of a businessman,

Gaines attended a highly ranked high school from which graduates became surgeons and ophthalmologists, research scientists and artists. After graduating from Rutgers with a degree in psychology, Gaines lived for a time in Manhattan with students attending Julliard, some of whom later became famous. Although he never saw the former Beatle, Gaines lived a few blocks from John Lennon's apartment. City life was not for him, however. "I used to go down to the river and watch the birds feeding and wonder how they could survive in the middle of all the pollution and industrialization," he said. "Watching them, I knew there was more to the life cycle than working and dying."

By the 1970s the West was not only urbanized but expensive, and the interior of the country promised more solitude and freedom. Gaines found out that a group from one of the State University of New York campuses had bought cheap land in West Virginia. In the midst of economic downturn, oil shortages, and a devastating war in Southeast Asia, he and his friends turned their backs on the consumerist, fossil fuel–based, competitive society and became homesteaders. Influenced by their example, in 1973 Gaines bought, with money saved from a job as a music therapist, thirty-four acres in Randolph County bordering the Monongahela National Forest in the Tygart River Valley and went there to live, taking only a few clothes and his mother's canning book from the 1940s.

The property began at the end of a four-mile-long gravel road. The right-of-way across the land—a narrow, steep, winding dirt road built by loggers—was difficult or impossible to drive over in bad weather, even with a four-wheel-drive vehicle. The closest village, Huttonsville, boasted two filling stations and a general store that sold seeds, fruits, vegetables, trousers, and shirts. The nearest town of any size—twenty-five miles away—was Elkins, the county seat, with ten thousand people. There were people living on a commune within ten miles, and there he met his future wife who had moved from Michigan with her two children. They married, Gaines adopted her children, and they set to work creating a homestead. Another son followed after five years and after three more another daughter, both born at home. At first, the family lived in an old house that had no electricity, running water, or furnace other than a wood-burning stove. Outside, half-concealed in the high grass, sat their predecessor's legacy, a wheelless '59 Chevy filled with empty wine bottles.

After a year they installed electricity in their old house, which allowed them to have a freezer, a radio, and lights, although there was still no plumbing. The first year they carried water from a stream. The well, which had been hand dug and lined with stone and tile, was contaminated from disuse. It took a year or so to learn how to clean it and be sure the water was safe to drink without boiling it. They washed clothes in an old wringer washer and hung them to dry in spring and summer. In autumn and winter they went to the laundromat in Elkins. Family members made gifts of sweaters and coats.

A few farmers made a meager living on the mountain, but homesteaders did not farm; instead, they gardened, growing every kind of vegetable and fruit the climate allowed: tomatoes, peppers, beans, corn, eggplant, melons, several types of winter and summer squash, okra, asparagus, potatoes, carrots, broccoli, apples, pears, cherries, strawberries, and raspberries. They made their own pickles and dried their own herbs. The orchard provided applesauce, apple butter, and cider, which they made with a press. "We spent all of September canning," Gaines said. "We canned over a thousand quarts of food every year, with over two hundred quarts of spaghetti sauce." They kept bees and collected honey which was their only source of sweetening. They also grew loofah gourds which, when dried, became sponges. Everything was recycled. Glass from the windows of a shack became glass for the windows of the house. Since they grew all their own food, there were no cartons or containers to discard, and so they generated no more than one bag of trash a year.

The property boasted two big barns and several small sheds where they kept chickens, ducks, goats, a cow, and a pony. One cow can produce more milk than a family needs, however, even with four children. They made butter, cheese, cottage cheese, and yogurt, and still had milk left over. On most farms, unused milk would be fed to the hogs (this practice led to the expression "slopping the hogs"), but the Gaineses were vegetarians, so they traded their excess milk for hay, grain, and straw.

Abundance created problems as well. Two ducks rapidly became forty ducks. The hens, however, were less practiced at hatching their eggs. So Gaines and his wife put the hen eggs into the duck nests; the eggs hatched, but the chicks followed the duck mothers to the pond where they stood on the edge and chirped. "Those chicks were never right in the head," he told me, "and we still had more ducks than we knew what to do with. Finally we broke our vegetarianism and ate them."

The woods provided wild plums, teaberries, chinquapins (related to chestnuts), walnuts, and blackberries. Neighbors taught them how and where to find mushrooms and the wild leeks called "ramps" that were tasty but smelly. One local dentist put a sign up in his office declaring that he would not work with anybody who'd eaten ramps within twenty-four hours.

"We used most of our time getting and preserving food," Gaines said, "and yet we spent more time as a family than most people ever do. Work and fun were the same. We were never afraid of going hungry or of being sick."

They cooked on a wood-burning stove, using logs gathered from the forest, first seasoning them and then splitting them to the size needed to fit. Hardwoods, especially oak and locust, provided most heat. Sycamore couldn't be split well. Poplar, on the other hand, burned too fast. Hickory burned well but did not give off as much heat. Nut and apple woods gave off the best aroma.

Calendars and watches proved superfluous: the thickness of morning fog in mid-April foretold a wet or dry summer; the family knew leeks were ripe when the spring days grew consistently warm; it was time to put the garden in when the apple trees blossomed. A damp, earthy smell in autumn signaled that mushrooms called "hen of the woods" were ready, growing at the base of an old-growth oak tree that was so big it took all the family members joining hands to encircle it. They needed no thermometers or barometers but learned to forecast rain from humidity and wind direction. A low-lying, heavy mountain fog in September signaled that they had two weeks to get their crops in.

"Our kids had no theater but they had a rich cultural experience," Gaines said. "The old radio was always tuned to NPR. Our bookshelves were filled with well-used copies of the classics that libraries had thrown out when they acquired new editions. We also got modern stuff like A Hitchhiker's Guide to the Galaxy. Our kids always read a lot and we read to them. I played guitar and flute and taught my kids to play. We spent evenings making our own music, playing and singing. Sometimes one of us read a book aloud to the whole family."

The mountains in some ways afforded more social life than New York had. A neighbor invited Gaines in to have biscuits and beans whenever he passed. She taught him much about gardening and shared a lifetime of experience on the mountain. Other neighbors were not so friendly. One man lived with a woman who had a daughter from a previous relationship. Years later, when he decided the girl was old enough, he kicked the mother out and forced the daughter to marry him. Belonging was not easy. The Gaineses went to a funeral of a woman who had lived near Huttonsville for sixty years, since her marriage at the age of eighteen. "Of course," a man remarked," she wasn't really from here. She was born south of here, in Webster County."

Guests were frequent, because the families from New York and Michigan visited often. "They thought we had lost our senses until they got here," Gaines said, "and then they thought we knew better than anyone else how to live. We never heard traffic because our house wasn't near a road. We never saw airplanes. I forgot they existed. We lived there thirteen years, from 1973 until 1986. I missed the end of the Vietnam War, the Carter years, much of the Reagan era. I was barely aware of him and didn't even know what he looked like. I hated the idea of 'I wish this day or week or month was over.' Every day was a new, un-planned experience, a chance to learn how to do something we hadn't done before. There was no such thing as inconvenience. Each new task was just part of life. It was a whole different way of thinking. We kind of knew what we were going to do each day, but no two days were ever the same." Life was like an old tale better told in the retelling.

Gaines and his wife built their own house, though it took nearly a decade to finish. "I had no reservations about build-ing my own house," he said, "although I'd never built anything, even in wood shop in school. But I knew that people had always built things, and I knew I could learn if I tried. You just pick up a hammer and you start." Materials came partly from whatever they could recycle and partly from a lumber mill, carried on foot to the property. The whole south wall was a series of win-dows constructed on the principle of solar heating. "On sunny days in winter you didn't need more than a very low fire, the house was so warm," Gaines said. "In summer we opened the windows, and the mountain breeze and tree canopy cooled the rooms." After the interior walls of the house were up, Gaines made all the furniture, including beds, tables, chairs, and cab-inets. When those were finished he added scroll work to all cabinet doors, table legs, and bedposts. He was still perfecting the woodwork when they left the house twelve years later.

For money, Gaines built and sold traditional lap dulcimers and hammer dulcimers and finally got a job playing and singing with a bluegrass band that performed at the Snowshoe and Sil-ver Creek Ski Resorts about twenty miles across the mountain. His wife worked as a teaching assistant in Mill Creek where their children went to school. But things were changing. The community broke up. One of the homesteaders who had bought very hilly land and who had terraced all his fields became a landscape gardener. The winters, which earlier had been lei-surely, became busier than summers. The bluegrass band began touring, first in West Virginia, then the eastern United States, and made and sold their records.

Gaines had built a life with low technology, but technology finally invaded the homestead. The family had no telephone for several years and no television until the last year they lived in Randolph County. Then the eldest son bought a TV set with money earned from a part-time job and carried it all the way from the road to the old house where he had taken up residence— "his" house, as he wanted to be independent. When the family began spending more and more evenings in the old house watching television, Gaines realized that his children needed and wanted a wider world than their homestead provided. "I had envisioned living there forever, with grandchildren bouncing on my knee," he said, but after his wife finished her degree in biology at Davis and Elkins College, they moved to Lewisburg where she attended the West Virginia College of Osteopathic Medicine. She eventually became a professor at Ohio University's medical college in Athens. Gaines, who had learned to read the natural world, finished his PhD in semiotics—the science of signs and one of the most arcane fields of communication. After twenty-four years of marriage, they divorced and sold the homestead as a vacation hunting lodge. Gaines went on to teach at Wright State University in Dayton and live in Yellow Springs, home of Antioch College—one of the most experimental colleges in the country—and has traveled widely in Southeast Asia and South America.

Perhaps they knew the meaning of Thoreau's conclusion upon leaving Walden Pond that he had "several more lives to live." The family had been part of the mountains, sunrises, birdsongs, seasons, spring floods, and autumn dry spells. They had raised four children. They were like rivers that change course and yet are the same rivers, flowing in different directions from the same sources.

Chapter Thirteen

Falling Rock Area

JEFFERSON COUNTY IS shaped somewhat like a keystone standing on its smaller end. The Ohio River separates it from the narrow peninsula of West Virginia and from Pennsylvania. Known
to locals as the tri-state area, the region is contained in the
Allegheny Mountain foothills drained by the river. Ice sheets
of the Wisconsinan glaciation 24,000 to 14,000 years ago that
crossed two-thirds of the state did not level Jefferson County's
hills. Yellow signs warning "FALLING ROCK" greet drivers on
roads walled in by stone. The culture leans toward the east: ed-
ucational television comes from Pittsburgh, the best newspaper
from Wheeling. During the mid-twentieth century, West Vir-
ginians commuted or moved to Ohio for jobs; people in Jefferson County reversed this trend and drove across the bridges to
Wheeling or Weirton to work in the mills, which, while dingy
and polluting, provided their laborers with a good living.

The most notable poet from the area, James Wright, fash-
ioned his artistic voice from the speech of the people of the
Ohio Valley and created a landscape, both industrial and pastoral, portraying the mill jobs as dead ends but presenting the
workers sensitively as fugitives in their own land. What Wright
captures so eloquently about that region, however, is the contrast between the dingy factories near whorehouses, slag heaps

left over from played-out mines, and lonely drunken itinerants with the fields and woodlands around them where "citizens" are farm animals and wildlife. Beyond the ugly industrial hell and the banal suburbs rise the beautiful forested hills—at least those not yet logged or mined. It is an ironic pastoral because it is overlooked, preserved more often by neglect than love.

The first white explorers in Jefferson County disembarked from a canoe as late as 1765, when Europeans had long penetrated regions farther west. The history of early settlement contains stories of eccentric people such as Joseph Ross who refused a congressional order to move until titles could be issued for the land he occupied. He, his wife, and son—the first white child born in Jefferson County, in 1784—lived inside a hollow sycamore. Joseph Ross died in 1806 when a tree limb fell on him. John Chapman (Johnny Appleseed) planted orchards near what is now George's Run. The meeting of European and native was bloody. Logan, a Delaware leader who had been friendly to whites until they began to take over, undertook raids referred to as Logan's Revenge after his family was murdered, but he was defeated in Dunmore's War. Cornplanter led his people against General Lewis in 1774. General Saint Clair's forces were defeated in 1794 and his own daughter kidnapped. When they found her, she had learned the native customs and skills at growing vegetables and making clothes. The mother and father of the Riley family were gathering sugar maple sap when they were attacked and killed by Indians. Their son James escaped by hiding in a horse trough, although two daughters were captured. After peace was declared, the commander at Fort Meigs gave James permission to look for his sisters. One had died; he found the other, who remembered her family but refused to return with her brother.

Another pioneer story of the eighteenth century involved James Maxwell, who headed west from Virginia, fought in Dunmore's War, and in 1780 brought a young bride to the farm near Rush Run, which he had cleared himself. At first the native people were friendly, but during an uprising they burned the Maxwells' cabin and kidnapped their baby girl. Maxwell's wife committed suicide with her husband's hunting knife, after which the farmer embarked on a terrorist rampage. While employed as a scout by Gen. "Mad" Anthony Wayne, Maxwell learned that his daughter was still alive and living with the Wyandots who called her "White Water Lily"; he secured her release and took her to live with him. She married a trader from Detroit, while Maxwell became a hard drinker in his later years. When his body was found floating in the river downstream from his old farm near Rush Run in the southern part of the county, no one could say whether his death was suicide or accident.

The county seat, Steubenville—named for the Revolutionary War general Friedrich Wilhelm von Steuben—enjoys the reputation of being a sort of smaller Youngstown run by organized crime and rife with bars, prostitution, and illegal gambling; as a child, however, I was unaware of organized crime and formed the impression that it was the churches that dominated. The city lies along the Ohio River and climbs the hills that rise from the valley. Until the advent of cheap imported steel, the town was kept alive by mills that sent their smokestacks into the air along the river (earning for the town the distinction of being the dirtiest municipality in the country in the 1960s). It seems dingy and run-down, but I think the Victorian houses and crumbling pavements give it a certain old-world charm, as did the horse trough alongside Market Street that stood until the road was widened into a four-lane highway.

I first learned to love the natural world when my father took my older sister and me for a walk in a cemetery near his boyhood home on Market Street, the main road into Steubenville from the west, and taught us the names of the flowers and plants. An ivy-covered stone cottage, now a historic dwelling, served as the caretaker's residence. Large trees shaded the entrance and several acres at the front. When the landscapers created the park, they left much of the area as it was, taking advantage of natural formations like stone outcroppings, slopes, and creeks. The cemetery thus looked more like a wild garden, reminding visitors of their cultural myth as well as the origin, sustenance, and conclusion of human lives. Once inside, the visitor was unaware of the busy city. Children rode their bicycles there because it was safer than the streets, and although people sometimes disapproved of those cyclists for laughing and shouting, they added the element of youth to a place preserved for memory and tradition and reminded us that the present and future are made of the past.

Just inside the iron gates, the lawn dipped to a creek along which grew flowering shrubs—rhododendron, forsythia, holly, lilac. Where the canopy was thinner, wild plants thrived—pink lady's thumb, orange forget-me-not, wild lily of the valley. As we walked farther, my father pointed out the black locust, oak, maple, poplar, tulip tree, sycamore, and willow. I began to see beyond the shady mass to the shape of leaves, texture of bark, variations of color. He reached down and pointed out tiny bluebells nearly out of sight beneath mayapple leaves. In the newer part of the cemetery, the trees were fewer and smaller, the landscaping more recent, and the birdsong less varied. Many indigenous plants survive in our time in part because of old cemeteries where every bit of ground has not been plowed, paved, or mowed. Trees and wildflowers provide evidence of the epochs of the forest; if they are destroyed, history will be destroyed with them.

My father had good reason to know well that cemetery in Steubenville. He had grown up in a large, multigenerational house, the veranda of which looked over the park. They had two outbuildings—a barn, which served by that time as a garage, and a livestock shed, which had been converted into a hatchery—on about half an acre of land. Behind the barn my grandmother grew flowers, kale, pumpkins and other squash, gourds, grapes, elderberries, apples, and cherries. My great-grandmother, grandmother, grandfather, great-aunt, and great-uncle—who had grown up on farms—lived most of their lives there. In later years, all were buried in that cemetery, but not before the city had appropriated houses, lawn, outbuildings, orchard, and garden—as well as a sizeable corner of the cemetery park—to widen the road that passed in front of the house and make a cloverleaf interchange. Their descendants have all left the area.

For forty years my parents lived in a farmhouse among hills to the west; although I lived there only eight years, I still refer to it as "home" because I believe that, for all our wanderings, home is the place that forges our character. The owner had sold the hundred or so acres around the house to a contractor, one of those people now called "developers" who buy up land from retiring farmers and subdivide it. He did not begin to build immediately, however, and during the first few summers we lived there, I rode ponies boarded on his land. I also wandered in his woods, which included a rock ledge we called a "cave" and waterfall. The best season was the autumn when the leaves turned red and gold, and puffballs on fallen tree trunks spouted golden dust when I touched them.

Some years later I returned from school to find a section of the woods ripped up by bulldozers. In a single afternoon about fifteen acres of large trees had been toppled and lay on their sides, enormous roots exposed and still clinging to hideous ripped-up clods of earth. Even the crime of the pioneers' clearing old-growth forest did not seem as bad as this. They at least worked hard to fell trees by hand. I walked among the trunks like battlefield dead, bitter about the maliciousness of destruction. Still, the land was not immediately developed; the owner, a cattle breeder, fenced it off and reseeded it to increase the grazing land for his Herefords. He even left about twenty of the largest trees standing. It looked bucolic for several decades before he finally sold it off in lots where people built what were then called "monster houses" but which are now common. Suburbanization increased even as the population of the area declined. Despite their apparent affluence, residents used the woods as a dump rather than pay anyone to haul away their trash.

Contractors posed a smaller threat to countryside and forests than strip mining, which desecrated more acreage in Jefferson than in any other county in the state. Anyone growing up in eastern Ohio is familiar with it. Strip-mining "shovels" are machines as big as small houses with "buckets" large enough for people to stand in. They devour whole landscapes in order to lay bare the coal that lies near the surface—and in doing so release toxic runoff. Vegetation grows back, however—first shrubby hawthorn and hardy grasses, then black locust and wild cherry trees. My friends and I liked to ride horses on land that had been strip-mined, referred to as "the strips," because we never had to be afraid of traffic or of anyone stopping us: no one cared what you did on those despoiled moonscapes. By the 1970s bituminous, or high-sulfur, coal, the type mined almost everywhere in Ohio, was already being vilified as the cause of acid rain that was killing the forests of New England. I assumed that strip mining was on its way out.

I was wrong. Years later as I was driving west on Route 22, I looked up to see a vista I had loved for years, four layers of wooded hills rising blue on paler blue in the distance. In a landscape like that, one could believe in eternity or in a garden that was the source of all life. The view had changed, however. The bucket of a strip-mining shovel was just barely visible beyond the last ridge. The next time I traveled that road, the hills had been stripped of trees and leveled.

According to state laws enacted in 1977, strip-mined land must now be "reclaimed." The strip pits are bulldozed over and landscaped, and sometimes even sculpted back into hills, although not the jagged steeps they once were. A local can tell always which slopes are natural and which are reclaimed strip land. The reclaimed ones have rounded tops, some of them dotted with sheep or cattle. They are seeded and sometimes planted with trees, and so if left alone they may become forests again.

Since I grew up during the movement to restore strip-mined areas and celebrated the passage of the federal Clean Air and Clean Water Acts (1970 and 1977), I believed people were going to reverse the trend toward exploitation of the earth. In 2012 I learned how wrong I was. Jefferson County sits over the Marcellus Shale, rich in natural gas and oil, and is once again being desecrated, this time by horizontal hydraulic fracturing, a technology in which millions of gallons of water and hundreds of thousands of gallons of toxic chemicals (including carcinogens, endocrine disruptors, and neurotoxins) are pumped at high pressure into drilled wells in order to release gas and oil. About 20 percent of this toxic water flows back to the surface along with mud contaminated with volatile organic compounds and must be stored in tanks or injected into old wells which have been known to leak. High-pressure injection also causes earthquakes. Compressor stations that process the gas continuously emit methane, a greenhouse gas twenty times more potent than carbon dioxide. Each frack requires hundreds of trips by heavy trucks, which damage roads and increase noise and pollution. Toxic spills and criminal dumping have been recorded in every state with fracking operations. While energy companies sometimes commit to repairing damaged roads and have been forced to pay the costs of toxic spills, they do not bear the health costs of polluted air, and only after extended lawsuits by landowners whose wells have been contaminated will they pay the costs of polluted water. Once containing the largest amount of strip-mined acreage in the state, Jefferson County now has the third-largest number of horizontal gas wells. Texas-based companies do most of the drilling and reap most of the profits.

Harrison County to the west of Jefferson County has also seen its share of deforestation, strip mining, and horizontal fracturing. In 2016, as part of the National Day of Action on Fracking, I visited Bluebird Farm near Tappan Lake, where a man named Mick Luber bought sixty-five acres in the back-to-the-land days of the 1970s—largely second-growth forest—and began an organic egg and produce operation using hand tools, self-built greenhouses, natural fertilizer, and ecological pest control. Believing (as I had) that the era of exploitation was over, he made a living selling organic produce to specialized markets in Wheeling and Pittsburgh. As always, however, Satan appears in paradise: in 2015 the farm was threatened by the Kinder-Morgan Company's plan to build a pipeline—ironically named Utopia—through Bluebird

Farm, which would have been acquired by eminent domain, even though the company is privately owned. Mick and his neighbors launched a campaign to stop the project, including front-page stories in the *Wheeling Intelligencer* and *Pittsburgh Press* and editorials on WWVA and KQED. They won, but only partly. Backing down before negative publicity, Kinder-Morgan agreed to reroute its pipeline, but the new route directly adjoins Bluebird Farm. The walker through deep woods listening to the songs of birds comes suddenly upon an enormous gorge carved through wooded hills to bury a twelve-inch steel pipe intended to transport ethylene and propane 270 miles to plastics manufacturing plants in Canada. Four miles from the farm, a compressor station stands on about ten acres carved from an otherwise bucolic landscape. Infrared photographs reveal what digital cameras cannot: these stations constantly emit large amounts of methane. Rural areas over shale deposits across the country have become "sacrifice zones" (a term used by the National Academy of Sciences and the Department of Interior) in which residents are considered expendable so that others in more populated places may live in the wasteful manner of contemporary America, just as those who lived downwind of atomic testing in the 1950s and 1980s were "expendable" in order that the United States might demonstrate worldwide military supremacy.

The shady dell where I first discovered the delight of the earth has been paved over; the forested hills that rose like an eternal promise are a stripped moonscape; the woods I explored on foot and on horseback are now used as trash dumps by the people who built houses on the fields; reclaimed strip mines are turned into toxic waste pits and pipeline corridors. Yet I remember that the second-growth woods sprang from the cut old-growth; the indigenous grasses that we pull from our gardens remind us that their seeds live on in the soil, however much of it has been transformed. Our bodies and our veins hold the remembrance

of what the land was and may be again if we can cease to think
of it in purely materialistic terms and accept it as a living thing.
The earth has made us what we are, sustains us, and will take us
back again when we have seen our share of passing seasons.

Chapter Fourteen

Preservation and Freedom

ON MY ROAD in Ashland County there are eight working family farms, but only two of them have no second income. Seven of the eight farms and much of the equipment were inherited, and the one that was purchased supplies only a small part of the owner's income. It is said that farmers live poor and die rich, for they sell wholesale and buy retail and are entirely subject to both weather and markets, but when they retire they sell their land at great profit for housing developments. No one wanting to begin farming for a living can afford to buy land because the subdivision of fields for housing, designed to attract high-income buyers, leads to inflated prices. The breaking up of farms, in turn, destroys the character of the countryside; thus realtors who promise their clients quiet and rural landscape annihilate the very thing they are selling. In his essay "Nature," Emerson rejoiced that although the land was owned by individual farmers, no one owned the landscape in his native Concord: "There is a property in the horizon which no man has but he whose eye can integrate all the parts, that is, the poet." In his essay "Walking," Henry David Thoreau, however, sounded the warning that before long the landscape itself would be owned and the land no longer worth traversing. His prophecy is fulfilled in our time when all value is measured in monetary terms, when the notion of "economy" includes only immediate fiscal concerns. He also wrote in *Walden* that a town is preserved not by its institutions but by the woods and swamps that surround it, but today I would reverse this tenet and declare that farmland and woods must be preserved by city dwellers who possess greater electoral clout than those in rural areas.

In the late 1990s, the Ashland County Planning Commission sponsored a series of talks on development. After presentations by a private company from Bowling Green, people divided into groups to discuss quality of life, transportation, and farmland preservation. At one large meeting, a wealthy realtor complained that planning would deprive people in his profession of their livelihood. I responded that our long-term quality of life was at stake: the county had almost nothing in the way of culture, but we had farmland, woods, and a landscape worth preserving. Realtors might be better off developing areas around existing villages.

We studied the experiences of communities like Yellow Springs, Ohio, where the Tecumseh Land Trust and other grassroots organizations have created the two-thousand-acre Jacoby Greenbelt in Miami Township targeted for preservation and where in 1999 a husband and wife who owned the historic Whitehall Farmhouse purchased, with help from nonprofit organizations, the rest of the 940-acre farm in order to prevent its being developed. More recently, in 2017, several residents and nonprofits have purchased the 267-acre Arnovitz Farm for the same reason. We also studied cities like Columbus with endemic urban sprawl, where, instead of renovating blocks of boarded-up houses, contractors built new housing developments that swallowed up open space, and new shopping centers meant that older ones turned into acres of crumbling concrete. The farmland preservation committee worked for a year to create a lengthy proposal calling for a trust that would allow landowners to place their farms voluntarily into a program that would prevent future development. Years after we presented our requests to the county commissioners, I met one of them on the street and asked whether anything had come of our proposal. He replied that perhaps farmland preservation should be the sphere of the Amish. Indeed, the commissioners rejected the proposals from all the planning committees.

What the county refused to do, however, the state accomplished in part, creating an easement program in which farmers who wanted to preserve their land could apply for 75 percent of the development rights and either donate the remaining 25 percent or apply for it from the county. Farmers could sell their land but not the development rights, and new owners could farm in any way they wished but could not subdivide the land or sell it for housing. At first the allocations went to the largest farmers, many of whom were already wealthy, but more recently some smaller farmers have been able to take advantage of the program.

Our township has the most varied landscape in the county and is the only one that still designates the best farmland as "prime." Some years ago a neighbor living across the road from us requested that the zoning of the entire township be changed to allow light industrial uses on land designated "general farm," the second most sensitive land use after "prime farm." He wanted to build a warehouse on his property, a reasonable plan in view of the fact that two warehouses already existed on our county road, one having been constructed before any of the land had been zoned, the other because an earlier commissioner neglected to follow the rules. The current, more responsible zoning commissioner, however, had refused the man's request for a variance, and hence the owner initiated this proposal to change the law itself. The commissioner congratulated the man on following the law (which others had not) but warned that any change could result in a plethora of warehouses going up all over the township. While this man's house and grounds always looked immaculate, if the law were to be changed, anyone who wanted to could apply for a permit to build a warehouse, and subsequent proposals might not come from such conscientious people.

The man's immediate neighbor alerted every property owner around him and many others, and all of us formed a committee called Keep Green Township Green. Farmers, nursery owners, small businesspeople, factory workers, lawyers, teachers, and one professor met to plan a strategy to prevent the change. We took our concerns to the township zoning commission and trustees in several meetings attended by county and township residents, with the extended family of the would-be warehouseman occupying one side of the room and the extended families of the neighbors on the other. The committee encouraged me to state the case for not changing the zoning laws. "You get up and talk," they'd say. "You're used to it."

At one of our task force meetings we learned that the would-be warehouseman had complained of someone shooting over his head to warn him not to pursue his venture. One man who lives just north of us, and the son of our place's previous owners, remarked, "It wasn't me. I know better than to shoot in the direction of a person." "It wasn't me," I replied. "I don't own a gun." "It wasn't me," retorted the salty, curmudgeonly farmer who had originally alerted us to the warehouseman's plan. "If it had of been me, I wouldn't't've missed."

The county planning commission voted heavily in favor of the variance, and four of five township zoning board members voted in favor. Finally, the Green Township trustees voted unanimously for it, after one of them declared that the concerns of the rest of us were "hot air." The township trustees, all longtime residents of the area, favored development, not preservation.

The members of Keep Green Township Green raised the necessary signatures and put the issue on the ballot, where the rezoning request was defeated two to one. The story does not end there, however; a year after this incident, someone else approached the commissioners with yet another request to change the allowable uses of general farm land, and still another landowner, a member of an old Green Township family and winner of the local county soil and water conservation award, requested to rezone his prime farm land in order to sell off a large parcel in housing lots. The argument that he should sell the best land and buy general farm acreage to develop met with hostility: he argued that the land was his to do with as he wished. The first of these requests was denied by the zoning board; the second was soundly defeated at the ballot box.

These victories seem miniscule, however, in view of the much greater threat presented by horizontal hydraulic fracturing. Gas wells drilled into the Utica Shale in 2012 by Devon Energy Corporation of Texas in Ashland and Knox Counties failed to produce the expected resources; environmentalists celebrated, thinking they were safe, especially when Devon and rival Chesapeake pulled their equipment out of the area. Celebrations were short-lived, however. In October 2017, massive, slow-moving vehicles spotted on the county and township roads turned out to be vibroseis trucks, also called "thumpers," that use sonar waves to detect the presence of mineral resources. While the companies that conduct these seismic surveys claim that sonar does not harm land or animals, people report feeling their houses shake; no reliable data exist concerning the effect on animals, and the waves have been known to crack the grout casing around well pipes. At the same time, Cabot Oil and Gas Corporation contacted local landowners about buying leases to fracture horizontally the Clinton Shale—a layer drilled vertically decades ago and much closer to the surface than either the Utica or Marcellus—and the Knox Dolomite Shale, which is much deeper (eight thousand feet in Ashland County). Poor well construction by Cabot in 2008–9 caused contamination of water wells in Dimock Township, Pennsylvania, one of the most notorious incidences of environmental damage caused by fracking. Recent innovations in the drilling process allow companies to extend their operations far beyond their 2012 capability: whereas the horizontal pipes in those days reached a mile, now they can travel four miles. When the process was first invented, each "frack" took about three million gallons of fresh water; now, each one requires about forty million, with the resultant increase in toxic flowback, and a well can be fracked multiple times. Residents have expressed alarm at the millions of gallons from the Black Fork River sold to Cabot by the Muskingum Watershed Conservancy District, the agency created to oversee water supplies and flood control. In addition to transmission pipelines, companies must construct "gathering lines," or shallow conduits that transport the resources locally; presently, no regulations exist in their construction or operation. Landowners who do not own the mineral rights to their property have no say in whether oil companies can drill beneath their land; local municipalities, furthermore, are prevented from banning, restricting, or regulating fracking by the Ohio Supreme Court ruling of 2015 upholding the state's exclusive right to regulate oil and gas exploration. Played-out gas wells may be sold to domestic or foreign companies for disposal of toxic fracking waste, creating increased risks of residential water-well contamination.

Although we believe that we live in a free society, we need to ask what we mean by freedom and whether progress (defined as industry and efficiency) and materialism should always be the defining goals. Realtors, developers, and industrialists argue that without "growth" the economy will collapse, but growth may be defined in ways other than increased development. Prosperity and freedom should mean more than ever-increasing income; they should also include the chance to engage in fulfilling work, the opportunity to pursue self-sufficiency, and the preservation of farmland and wilderness. Many countries with vibrant economies still preserve much that is valuable: Ireland protects farmland and subsidizes the rural way of life for which it is famous; public footpaths in Britain allow people to walk into the country where zoning prevents urban sprawl, and laws enable villages to maintain their local character; travelers on dusty roads in Italy pass vineyards nearly as old as their civilization.

In his essay "The Phenomenon of Placelessness," William Vaughan questions our willingness to consider values solely in economic terms, in which no relationship is forged between people and the natural world, and in which possession is a mere legality and not a living bond. He writes, "The claim to possess cannot grow out of a lived experience; it is an abstract legal claim, a construct established by social convention to order the life of the world or the world of artifacts." America is all about escaping the past and overcoming the circumstances of birth; land that has no value other than its price contains no meaning in personal history. This country, however, also claims to value independence that the yeoman farmer achieved and that is denied when "market forces" allow large growers and realtors to drive small producers out of business. No one is truly free who is dependent on others for food, clothing, shelter, water, or air; no one is truly free in a culture in which lawmakers do the bidding solely of their wealthy benefactors and in which the oldest and most important profession of civilized society, farming, can be practiced only by those who are independently wealthy or who inherit their land.

If preservation and desire for true freedom rather than merely personal profit helped to guide our policies—if we had the political will—we might adopt a "green" economy, including serious investment in sustainable energy such as solar, wind, hydro, and geothermal technologies, which would eliminate our dependence on extractive industries that produce huge amounts of hazardous waste, the worst being horizontal hydraulic fracturing and mountaintop coal mining. Commitment to public transportation, ordinances against excessive noise, expanded creation of parkland, downtown pedestrian areas, and regulations that prohibit development of open space until all available urban land is in use would make cities and towns desirable places to live and thus eliminate the need to "escape" to the suburbs. Architectural, sartorial, and horticultural compatibility with place; control of pollution by severely charging industry for its waste; and adoption of local, regional, and national policies that actively promote recycling and conservation would enable us to return to some measure of independence.

Like careless children who waste their inheritance, we do not deserve the planet we have been given. Instead of using water and land carelessly, we should consider them gifts given to us by the ice ages. We need to redefine "economy" and "freedom" to include the long-term ramifications of our actions. Our national goals should include more than addiction to ill-defined "progress," efficiency, and increasing materialism; they should include not only preserving but also revering our soil, air, and water, without which we cannot survive, much less prosper.

Bibliography

Works Cited

"Amish Farmers Fare Better than 'English,' Study Says." *Ashland Times-Gazette*, June 6, 2003, A1, A6.

Anderson, L., S. Slovic, and J. P. O'Grady, eds. *Literature and the Environment: A Reader on Nature and Culture*, 290–95. New York: Longman, 1999.

Bass, Rick. "Why I Hunt." *Sierra Magazine*, July/Aug. 2001, 58–61.

Berry, Wendell. *A Continuous Harmony: Essays Cultural and Agricultural*. New York: Harcourt, Brace, Jovanovich, 1972.

———. "The Wild." *Collected Poems*. New York: North Point, 1994.

Bromfield, Louis. *The Farm*. New York: Grosset & Dunlap, 1933.

———. *Malabar Farm*. New York: Ballantine, 1948.

———. *Pleasant Valley*. New York: Harper and Brothers, 1945.

Cronon, William, ed. "The Trouble with Wilderness; Or, Getting Back to the Wrong Nature." In *Uncommon Ground: Toward Reinventing Nature*, 69–90. New York: W. W. Norton, 1995.

Emerson, Ralph Waldo. "Nature." In *Selections from Ralph Waldo Emerson*, 21–56. Boston: Riverside Editions, 1957.

Finneran, Richard, J., ed. *The Collected Works of William Butler Yeats*, vol. 1, 215–17. New York: Macmillan, 1989.

Hillis, Newell Dwight. *The Quest of John Chapman: The Story of a Forgotten Hero*. New York: Grosset & Dunlap, 1908.

Hunt, Tim, ed. *The Collected Poetry of Robinson Jeffers*, vol. 1. Stanford: Stanford Univ. Press, 1988.

Jeffers, Robinson. "Bixby's Landing." In Hunt, *Collected Poetry of Robinson Jeffers*, 388.

———. "Shine, Perishing Republic." In Hunt, *Collected Poetry of Robinson Jeffers*, 15.

Kimmerer, Robin Wall. *Braiding Sweetgrass*. Minneapolis, MN: Milkweed Editions, 2013.

Kline, David. *Great Possessions: An Amish Farmer's Journal*. Wooster, OH: Wooster Book Company, 2001.

———. *Scratching the Woodchuck: Nature on an Amish Farm*. Athens: Univ. of Georgia Press, 1999.

Kumin, Maxine. In *Deep: Country Essays*. Boston: Beacon Press, 1988.

Leopold, Aldo. *A Sand County Almanac and Sketches Here and There*. New York: Oxford Univ. Press, 1989.

Loeffler, Lisa. "The FBI's file on Louis Bromfield." *Mansfield News Journal*, Aug. 22, 1999, 1A, 6A, 7A.

Matthiessen, Peter. *The Snow Leopard*. New York: Bantam, 1981.

Nissenson, Hugh. *The Tree of Life*. New York: Harper & Row, 1985.

Ohio Division of Geological Survey, 1998. Physiographic Regions of Ohio: Ohio Department of Natural Resources, Division of Geological Survey, page-size map with text, 2 p., scale 1:2,100,000.

Pershing, Henry A. *Johnny Appleseed and His Time: An Historical Romance*. Strasburg, VA: Shenandoah Publishing House, 1930.

Pollan, Michael. *The Botany of Desire: A Plant's Eye View of the World*. New York: Random House, 2002.

Price, Robert. *Johnny Appleseed: Man and Myth*. Gloucester, MA: Peter Smith, 1967.

Snyder, Gary. *The Practice of the Wild*. San Francisco: North Point Press, 1990.

Swedenborg, Emanuel. *Angelic Wisdom Concerning the Divine Love and the Divine Wisdom*. New York: Swedenborg Foundation, 1946. First published 1763.

———. *The Four Leading Doctrines of the New Church, Signified by the New Jerusalem in the Revelation: Being those Concerning the Land; the Sacred Scriptures; Faith; and Life*. New York: American Swedenborg Printing and Publishing Society, 1878.

———. *Heaven and Its Wonders and Hell*. New York: Swedenborg Foundation, 1938.

Thoreau, Henry David. *Walden and Other Writings by Henry David Thoreau*. New York: Modern Library, 1965.

Vaughan, William. "The Phenomenon of Placelessness." In *Essays on Heidegger and European Philosophy: Meridian Thinking*, 260–71. Lewiston, NY: Mellen Press, 2002.

Williams, Ted. "Natural Allies." *Sierra Magazine*, Sept./Oct. 1996, 47–53, 69.

Zuck, Barbara. "A Hunting We Will Go." *Capitol Magazine*, Dec. 6, 1987.

Works Consulted

Alessio, Liz. "Johnny Appleseed Days: The Man behind the Myth." *Ashland Times-Gazette*, Sept. 28, 2000, C1.

Anderson, David D. *Louis Bromfield*. New York: Twayne, 1964.

———. "Louis Bromfield and Ecology in Fiction: A Re-Assessment." *Midwestern Miscellany* 25 (1997): 48–57.

———. "Louis Bromfield, Nature Writer and Practical Ecologist." *Society for the Study of Midwestern Literature* 27, no. 3 (Fall 1997): 11–16.

———. "Louis Bromfield's 'Cubic Foot of Soil.'" *Midwestern Miscellany* 27 (Spring 1999): 41–47.

———. "Louis Bromfield's Myth of the Ohio Frontier." *Old Northwest: A Journal of Regional Life and Letters* 68 (1980): 63–74.

———. "Midwestern Writers and the Myth of the Search." *Georgia Review* 34 (1980): 131–43.

———. "The Search for a Living Past." In *Sherwood Anderson: Centennial Studies*, edited by Hilbert H. Campbell and Charles E. Modlin, 212–23. Troy, NY: Whitson, 1976.

Bachchan, Harbans Rai. *W. B. Yeats and Occultism*. New York: S. Weiser, 1974.

Berlin, Jeremy. "So That's Why the Long Face." *National Geographic* 232, no. 4 (Oct. 2017).

Bratton, Daniel. "Edith Wharton and Louis Bromfield: A Jeffersonian and a Victorian." *Edith Wharton Review* 10, no. 2 (Fall 1993): 8–11.

Bresnahan, Roger J. "The Village Grown Up: Sherwood Anderson and Louis Bromfield." *MidAmerica: The Yearbook of the Society for the Study of Midwestern Literature* 12 (1985): 45–52.

Brown, Morrison. *Louis Bromfield and His Books*. Fair Lawn, NJ: Essential Books, 1957.

"Burning of the Maxwell Cabin." *Jefferson County Historical Association Newsletter* 34, no. 2 (June 14, 2017): 6.

Cowley, Malcolm. *Exile's Return: A Literary Odyssey of the 1920s*. New York: Viking, 1965.

Derrenbacher, Merle. "Louis Bromfield: A Bibliography." *Bulletin of Bibliography* 17 (1942): 141–45.

Eppard, Philip B. "Louis Bromfield." In *American Writers in Paris, 1920–1939*, edited by Karen Lane Rood, 58–60. Detroit: Thomson Gale, 1980.

Farb, Peter. *Man's Rise to Civilization: The Cultural Ascent of the Indians of North America*. New York: Penguin, 1978.

Gross, W. H. "Lake Park Expansions." *Ohio Cooperative Living* (May 2018): 20D–20E.

Grover, Dorys Crow. "Four Midwestern Novelists' Response to French Inquiries on Populism." *MidAmerica: The Yearbook of the Society for the Study of Midwestern Literature* 18 (1991): 59–68.

———. "Louis Bromfield in France." *MidAmerica: The Yearbook of the Society for the Study of Midwestern Literature* 24 (1997): 115–21.

Harper, Arthur R. *Ohio in the Making: A Brief Geological History of Ohio.* Columbus: Ohio State Univ. Press, 1948.

Hatton, Robert W. "Louis Bromfield Revisited." *Ohioana Quarterly* 23 (1980): 48–54.

"Historic Marker Unveiled." Newsletter, Seedlings (Johnny Appleseed Heritage Center and Outdoor Drama) 1, no. 4 (Nov. 2000): 2.

Hough, Jack L. *Geology of the Great Lakes.* Urbana: Univ. of Illinois Press, 1958.

Hughes, James M. "The Central Blank: Louis Bromfield and Ohio." *Ohioana Quarterly* 20 (1977): 111–13.

"Johnny Appleseed in Central Ohio." Pamphlet. Columbus: Ohio Historical Society, n.d.

Johnny Appleseed, Orchardist. Fort Wayne, IN: Fort Wayne Public Library, n.d.

Kehoe, Terence. *Cleaning Up the Great Lakes: From Cooperation to Confrontation.* DeKalb: Northern Illinois Univ. Press, 1997.

Knepper, George W. *An Ohio Portrait.* Columbus: Ohio Historical Society, 1976.

Lafferty, Michael B. *Ohio's Natural Heritage.* Columbus: Ohio Academy of Science, n.d.

Llona, Victor. "Literary Gardeners: Louis Bromfield and Jean de Boschère." *Laurels* 59, no. 2 (Fall 1988): 101–10.

Marriot, Alice Lee. *American Indian Mythology.* New York: Mentor, 1968.

McMurty, Richard Keith. *John McMurty and the American Indian: A Frontiersman in the Struggle for the Ohio Valley.* Berkeley, CA: Current Issues Publications, 1980.

Muskingum Watershed Conservancy District. "History." https://www.mwcd.org/get-to-know-us/history.

National Toxic Land/Labor Conservation Service. "National TLC Service Established." Posted May 1, 2011. http://www.nationaltlcservice.us/2011/05/national-tlc-service-established/.

Oslin, Irv. "Brinkhaven to Mohawk Dam Most Pristine Stretch of River." *Ashland Times-Gazette,* July 29, 2014.

———. "Paddling Clear Ford Can Be Rewarding Experience." *Ashland Times-Gazette,* Sept. 11, 2014.

———. "Rewards Await Paddlers beyond Frye's Landing." *Ashland Times-Gazette,* July 28, 2014.

Pickren, Graham, ed. *Engagement* (blog). "The Sacrifice Zones of American 'Energy Independence': Pipeline and Refining Expansion in the Chicago Region," Aug. 16, 2018. https://aesengagement.wordpress.com/2018/08/16.

Sams, Dylan. "Oil, Gas-Seeking Trucks Spotted near Perrysville." *Ashland Times-Gazette*, Oct. 13, 2017.

Sherman, Thomas Fairchild. *A Place on the Glacial Till*. New York: Oxford Univ. Press, 1996.

US Environmental Protection Agency. "Hydraulic Fracturing for Oil and Gas: Impacts from the Hydraulic Fracturing Water Cycle on Drinking Water Resources in the United States (Final Report)." 2016. https://cfpub.epa.gov/ncea/hfstudy/recordisplay.cfm?deid=332990.

Vanderwerth, W. C., ed. *Indian Oratory: Famous Speeches by Noted Indian Chieftains*. Norman: Univ. of Oklahoma Press, 1971.

Waterman, Jayne. "Louis Bromfield and the Idea of the Middle." *Mid-America: The Yearbook of the Society for the Study of Midwestern Literature* 30 (2003): 73–85.

Wilson, Edmund. "What Became of Louis Bromfield?" *New Yorker* (Apr. 1, 1944): 20.

Index

Page numbers in bold refer to illustrations.